# Dedication

This book is dedicated to the Lord who gave me the talent and has blessed me by allowing me to make a living doing something I love.  I strive to thank Him by portraying the beauty and magnificence of His Creation.

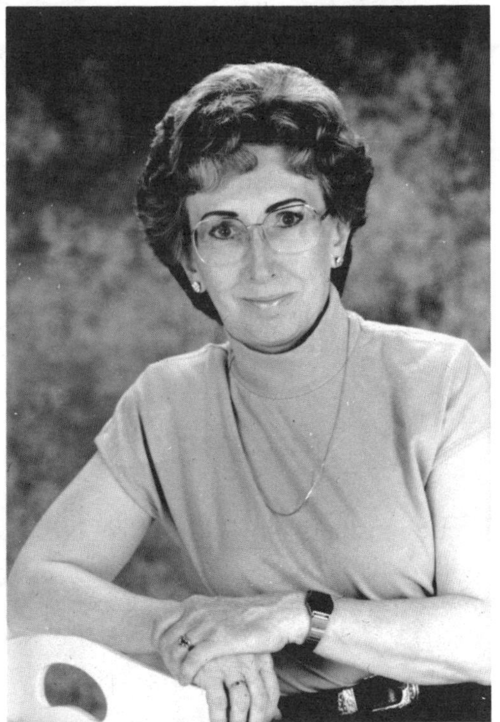

# About the Author

I was born in Montana, but have lived in Seattle, Washington most of my life. Early exposure to the wonderful variety of nature in the Pacific Northwest has definitely had an influence on my painting.

I have enjoyed drawing and other artistic pursuits since I was a small child.  Drawing classes in high school and college gave me a good foundation.  I started painting in 1974 when I took a class at a local recreation center.  After that I attended painting classes at an art store and then took workshops from many different Northwest artists.  I have developed my technique in flowers primarily on my own.

As you can see, my style is realistic and detailed.  I strive to capture the magic of light and shadow.  I enjoy a variety of subjects from mountains, seascapes, waterfalls and florals to an occasional still life or portrait. The inspiration for my painting comes from skiing, hiking and traveling locally and abroad.  I work largely from photos that my husband and I take, though I may use only a portion of a photo or combine many photos into one painting.

I teach workshops at various studios and stores around the Pacific Northwest.  I sell my paintings and prints of them mostly through mall shows in Washington State and occasionally in galleries. My work is included in collections throughout the United States as well as in England, Australia and New Zealand.

# *Supplies*

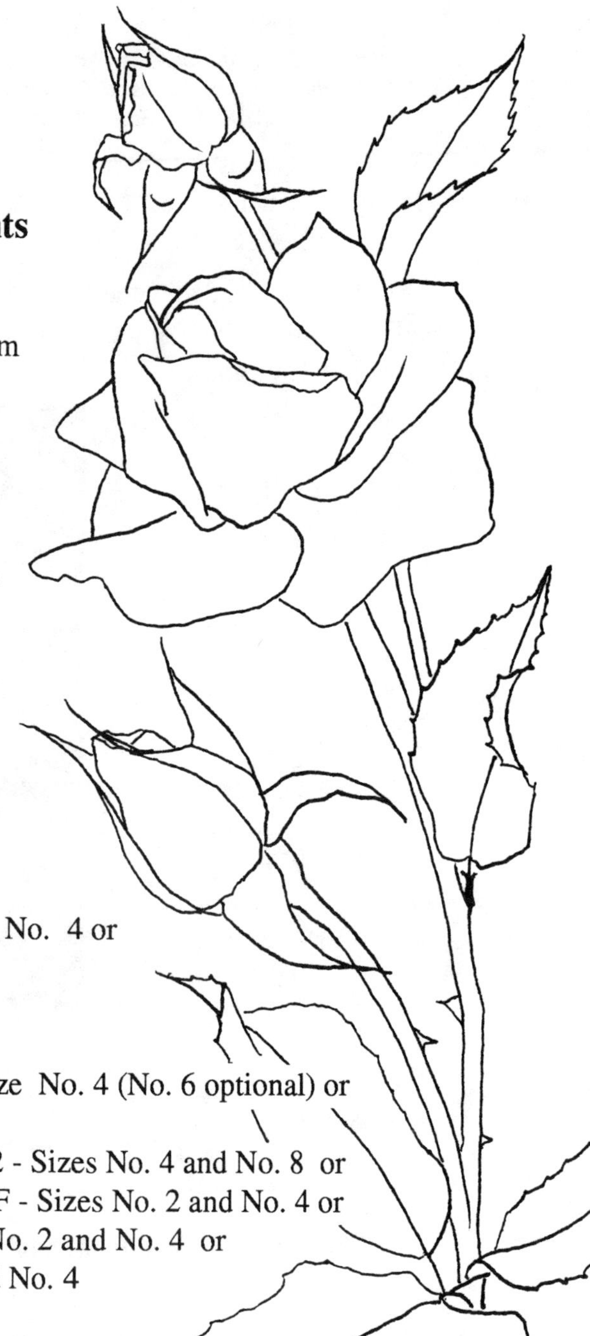

## PALETTE - Oil Paints

White - I prefer Grumbacher Original Formula Titanium

| | |
|---|---|
| Zinc Yellow | Cadmium Yellow Pale |
| Cadmium Yellow Light | Cadmium Yellow Medium |
| Naples Yellow | Yellow Ochre |
| Raw Sienna | Cadmium Orange |
| Cadmium Red Light | Cadmium Red Medium |
| Grumbacher Red | Thalo Red Rose |
| Alizarin Crimson | Thio Violet |
| Cerulean Blue | French Ultramarine Blue |
| Viridian | Burnt Sienna |
| Burnt Umber | Ivory Black |

## WEBER PERMALBA COLORS

| | |
|---|---|
| Yellow Citron | Leaf Green Medium |
| Terre Verte (Avoid Substitutes) | |

## BRUSHES

**Liners:**

Grumbacher Control Plus Long Liners No. 7801 - Size No. 4 or
Robert Simmons F51 - Folk Artist Liner No. 4

**Small "Mock Sables":**

Cat's Tongue - Grumbacher Control Plus No. 7805 - Size No. 4 (No. 6 optional) or
    similar cat's tongue brush
Flats - Grumbacher Control Plus Flat Shaders No. 7802 - Sizes No. 4 and No. 8 or
    Grumbacher Bristlette (white nylon) No. 4720-F - Sizes No. 2 and No. 4 or
    Loew-Cornell White Nylon No. 797-F - Sizes No. 2 and No. 4 or
    Winsor & Newton UNIVERSITY F - No. 2 and No. 4
Round - Raphael No. 8676 Size No. 4 (sable) or
    Winsor & Newton Round Series 233 - Size No. 3 or
    Loew- Cornell No. 797-R (white nylon) Size No. 2

**Small Fans:**

Robert Simmons White Bristle No . 448 - Size No. 2 or No. 3 or
Loew-Cornell White Bristle No. 32 - Size No. 2 or No. 3
Optional - Sable or Badger Fan such as - Richeson Series 9451 No. 2

**White Bristle Brushes:**

Flats and/or Filberts Sizes 2 or 3, 4, 5, 6, 8 and 10 such as:
Grumbacher Gainsborough Series No. 1271-F or
Grumbacher Edgar Degas Series No. 4229
Mop brush such as Winsor & Newton Series 240 NJ - Size 1

**Other:**

"Bush Brushes" - Older brushes that have gotten bushy - small and medium

# MISCELLANEOUS

12 x 16 Palette Paper Pad
Odorless Thinner and Container
Liquin (Winsor & Newton prepared medium)
Medium (1/2 Linseed or Stand Oil + 1/2 Thinner or prepared medium <u>without</u> a drier) and container
Paper Towels (I like Job Squad)
Non-linty Rags (<u>old</u> sheet torn up works well)
Tracing Paper
Graphite Paper (black or grey and white)
Palette Knife to mix with
Tweezers (for getting lint, hairs, etc. off canvas)
Soft Eraser such as Pink Pearl
Ruler
Extra container for clean thinner to clean off black and grey canvas

# CANVAS

I paint exclusively on a nylon canvas called Artist Dream Canvas. It has a wonderfully smooth surface which makes it much easier to paint all the details I like to do. I particularly like the glow or luminescence of the colors on this canvas. It uses a little less paint and also dries faster than cotton or linen canvas. A "plus" is that it can be used with any medium - oil, watercolor, acrylic, pen and ink or pastels! It comes already stretched and primed in white, black or grey.

For information on where to buy the canvas contact:

**ARTISTIC ACCENTS - MORGAN SCHOOL OF FINE ART**
16023 - 252nd Avenue S.E.
Issaquah, WA  98027
(206) 313 - 5979

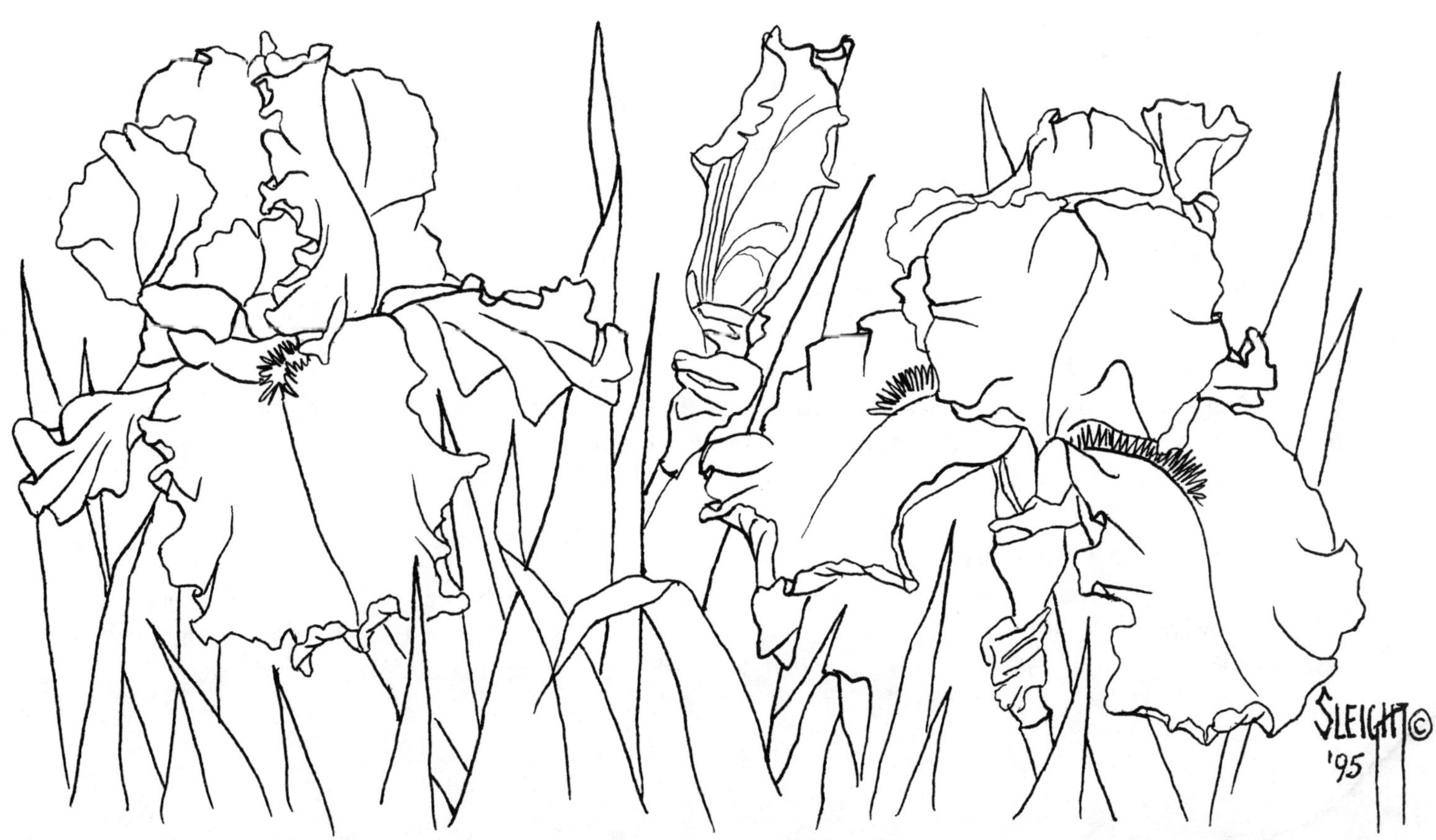

# Definition of Terms

**BACKLIGHT:**

Reflected light on the shadow side of an object (usually blue on outdoor scenes).

**BASECOAT OR UNDERCOAT:**

A relatively thin layer of paint (but not a wash) usually put on with medium or Liquin into which other colors are added for shading.

**BUSH BRUSH:**

An old flat bristle or larger mock sable brush that is "bushy".

**CAST SHADOWS:**

Shadows that are cast on an object because another object (such as a tree, petal or leaf) is blocking out the light source.

**CALYX:**

The outside - green part of a rosebud (also visible on the underside of full blooms).

**GLAZING:**

Paint added over the top of dry paint and applied with enough medium to make it somewhat transparent, allowing the paint underneath to show through.

**HIGHLIGHTING:**

Adding the brightest and lightest areas to an object.

**LIP OF PAINT:**

A line or edge of paint that has thickness.

**MINI-FAN BRUSH:**

A small fan brush made from your long liner brush by pressing the wet bristles between your thumbnail and forefinger to spread them out.  See illustration in front of book.

**MOCK SABLE BRUSH:**

A synthetic brush such as a nylon or similar soft fiber other than sable.

**PUNCHING IN OR TAPPING:**

A stroke usually using a "bush" brush that is aimed straight at the canvas with the tail of the brush pointed slightly upward so that only the upper portion of the bristles make contact with the canvas.  See illustration in front of book.

**SOFTENED PILE OF PAINT:**

A pile of highlight color to which a small amount of medium (linseed oil + thinner) has been added and mixed well with the knife.  It is essential that this be mixed evenly.  Enough medium should be added that the paint will not hold peaks when the knife is pulled straight up from the pile.

# Waterdrops

Water has no color of its own - it takes on the color of whatever it's on.  If the waterdrop is on a green leaf, it is painted with darker and lighter shades of green.  If it's on a pink flower, it's painted with darker and lighter shades of pink.

It is easiest to do the waterdrops when your painting it completely dry.  That way if you don't like what you've done, you can remove it with thinner and try again.

Remind yourself of the direction of light in your painting.

**STEP 1:**

Using a small liner brush and thinner, paint the top of the drop nearest the direction of light (and the "tail" if it's running) with a darker shade of the petal or leaf color that it is on.  Don't get it too dark - just dark enough to show up.  On a white or very light pastel petal, make your color a greyer shade of the petal color.

Paint the shadow under the drop and on the opposite side from the light with this same dark (or grey) color.  The shadow may occasionally be darker than the color at the top of the drop.

**STEP 2:**

Paint the inside of the bottom of the drop (just above the shadow) with a lighter shade of the petal or leaf color that it is on.  This color is usually the mixture you used for highlights.

Use a dry brush (usually a liner brush) to blend the dark and light colors within the drop together.  On a very large waterdrop there may be leaf or petal color showing in the middle.

**STEP 3:**

Add the spot of highlight (light reflecting off the surface of the water) over the dark area on the side <u>nearest</u> the light.  Lay the tip of your liner brush horizontally into a pale mixture of white + yellow (whatever yellow you are using in that painting).  Pull straight up until a tail forms on the tip of the brush (see illustration).  Touch just this tail to the canvas to form the highlight.

# Suggestions

1.  Try to cluster the drops rather than spreading them out evenly like polka dots.
2.  An odd number of drops is best, though if one is a distance from the others, it is possible to have an even number.
3.  Pay attention to the angle of the leaf or petal the drop is on.  If the leaf or petal is seen at an angle, the drop cannot be round - it must be oval.  (It might be round if you are looking straight down on it, but would not appear so if seen at an angle).  You can have a round drop on a leaf or petal that is facing you.
4.  Place your drops nearer the middle of the painting rather than the edges.  If possible, place them to  lead the eye to the center of interest.  Be sure not to put two drops horizontally across from each other - they will look like eyes!

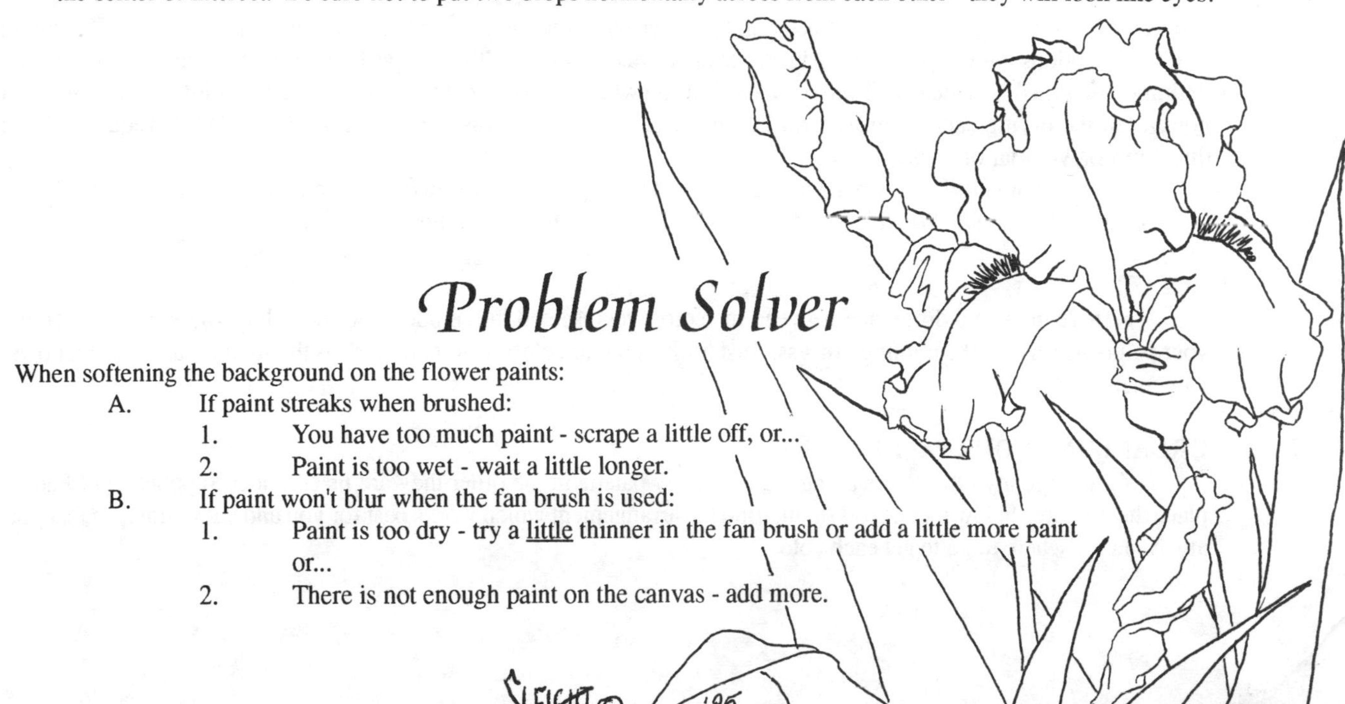

# Problem Solver

When softening the background on the flower paints:
- A.    If paint streaks when brushed:
  1.    You have too much paint - scrape a little off, or...
  2.    Paint is too wet - wait a little longer.
- B.    If paint won't blur when the fan brush is used:
  1.    Paint is too dry - try a <u>little</u> thinner in the fan brush or add a little more paint or...
  2.    There is not enough paint on the canvas - add more.

# General Information

**LIGHTING:**

One of the first things you should do when starting a painting is to determine the light source (which direction the light is coming from). Keep this in mind throughout the painting so you will get your shadows and highlights in the proper places.

**MIXING:**

On each set of directions you will find a list of the colors you need to mix - some before you start painting, some as you progress through the painting. For some of the floral paintings, you will need to do most of the mixing before you start, since most of the mixes are needed in the background.

When mixing, the first color listed is the one you start with and the one you use the most of. The last color listed is the one you need least of. When mixing combinations that are new to you, always start cautiously - it's easier to add more color than to correct it if you get too much.

A note on the green mixes: The five or six green mixes you see in the sample are the ones I use for most of my paintings. I sometimes mix them a little bluer or a little greener, but for this book I have made most of them the same for your ease in mixing.

When you mix the Leaf Green + Blue mixture (dk. green No. 2), make quite a large pile of it. Then separate the pile into two piles - one having the amount listed for dk. green No. 2. The other pile is what you make the med. green No. 1 out of (add White and Yellow Citron). When that one is mixed, divide that pile in two and mix med. green No. 2 from one of these. Repeat this for the highlight green.

The measurements that you see after the names of the mixes for each painting are the <u>approximate</u> amounts of that mix you will need to complete that painting. This will vary some from person to person depending on how much paint you use. You don't need to actually measure the paint - just use it as a guide to which mixes you need a lot of and which you need very little of.

**PROGRESSION ON A PAINTING:**

On landscapes and seascapes I always start at the top and work downward through the painting, usually finishing what is in back before I put something in front of it. For flowers, I always finish the blurry background (except on black canvases) first, <u>leaving base canvas where the foreground flowers and leaves will be.</u> When I start on the foreground, I generally start on the upper left simply because I am right-handed and I like to have a clean spot to rest my little finger to steady my hand! (If you are left-handed, you might want to start on the upper right for the same reason.)

**MEDIUMS:**

Many students seem to be confused about when to use a medium and when not to. A medium can be used when painting over bare (or dry) canvas. When painting over wet paint, no medium is necessary since there is wet paint underneath. Exceptions are when you are using your liner brush to draw with (such as branches) or when you are glazing (see definition of terms). Which medium to use depends on whether you want the paint to remain wet longer (use one that does <u>not</u> hasten the drying such as linseed oil mixtures) or to dry faster (use one with a drier added or Liquin). Read the directions on your jar of medium.

Throughout this book, when I say "medium" I am referring to the linseed oil and thinner mixture (described under Miscellaneous Supplies). When I want you to use Liquin, I will say "Liquin".

**COLORS:**

There may be a difference between the colors represented in the book and the colors you will get when mixing your paints because of the printing process. Just try to get your colors as light or dark as the samples and use your own best judgement.

**ORGANIZING YOUR PALETTE:**

I arrange my tube colors along the top of my palette in the order they are listed under Supplies - Oil Paints, and place the mixtures below them. You should find the arrangement which works best for you and stick with it so that you will always know where to go to get each color.

**STAYING CLEAN:**

This is more than just neatness -it is best for your health (toxic ingredients in the paints can be absorbed through the skin) and for your painting.  I am frequently asked how I stay so clean when I paint!  I have two basic rules.:

1.  Never put down a dirty brush - always clean it first.
2.  Don't hold your paper towel or rag in your hand - put it in a corner of your palette or on your table or easel.

Also, try using baby wipes (especially those with lanolin in them) to clean your hands instead of paint thinner - much better for your health!

**LINER BRUSH:**

Many students have trouble making a fine line and getting a fine tip on the end of branches.  Always use a little thinner with your paint and roll the brush in the paint mixture to get a good point on it for "drawing".  If you mix the thinner in with your brush, you may need to clean the brush and then pick up the paint with it.  When you want a thicker line, press harder with the brush; when you want a fine tip, pull the brush away from the canvas releasing pressure as you get to the tip.  Practice on your palette.

**FLAT VS. FILBERT BRUSH:**

When applying paint or blending with a flat brush, the brush should be pointed straight at the canvas.  When applying paint or  blending with a filbert (or cat's tongue) brush, the side of the bristles should be used instead of the end.  See illustration in front of book.

**DARKS AND LIGHTS:**

When trying to make some part of a painting look lighter, instead of adding more white, try darkening behind or next to the area.

# General Directions for Flowers

My progression for flowers is as follows:

First I paint the background (except for black canvases), leaving the canvas bare where the foreground flowers and leaves will be.  Note that the darks in the background are placed next to light areas in the foreground, and light areas in the background are placed next to dark areas in the foreground.  Then I brush the background with a fan brush to blur it and straighten the brush strokes out. Next I clean out any paint that has streaked over the foreground flowers and leaves using a flat mock sable brush and thinner.

I put a basecoat of paint on several petals (or an entire bud) using the middle tone of the color for each petal (not the darkest or the lightest) and some Liquin.  It is essential to keep this paint smooth - no texture - but not too thin.  I leave tiny cracks where my lines are, unless I see them through the paint.  Then I do a small amount of shading with darker colors.  Next I brush each petal lightly with my small fan brush.  Then I let this paint dry a little while I put a basecoat on more petals or leaves.

I go back to the first petals when the paint is getting sticky and add more darks and shadows, working them into the basecoat.  It is very important to do this before the paint dries completely! (If the paint is too dry, I add a little more Liquin; if it is completely dry, I start over again with the basecoat).  At this stage, it is important to note that the petals will not be as bright as in the picture, because no highlights have been added yet.  Then I brush each petal lightly again with the small fan brush in the direction it is curving or the direction the veins would be if you could see them.

Before doing the shading on the next set of petals, I put a basecoat on more petals or leaves so they can be drying a little while I am working on other areas.  Proceed in this fashion throughout the painting, always having something drying (to the sticky stage) while you are working shadows on others.  However, don't put a basecoat on more than you will be able to finish in one day, since it is very difficult to shade or highlight dry petals.

When the darker shades have been added on one flower or a segment of one, then I add the highlights.  This is done with a softened pile (see Definition of Terms) of the highlight color which is applied with the liner brush.  Then this highlight is brushed lightly with the "mini-fan" (see Definition of Terms).  Some extra darks can be added where necessary with the liner brush.

After all the flowers and leaves are done, I add any cast shadows that are needed.  These can also be glazed on when the painting is dry.  Then I put the waterdrops on (see Waterdrop Instructions).

# *Illustrations*

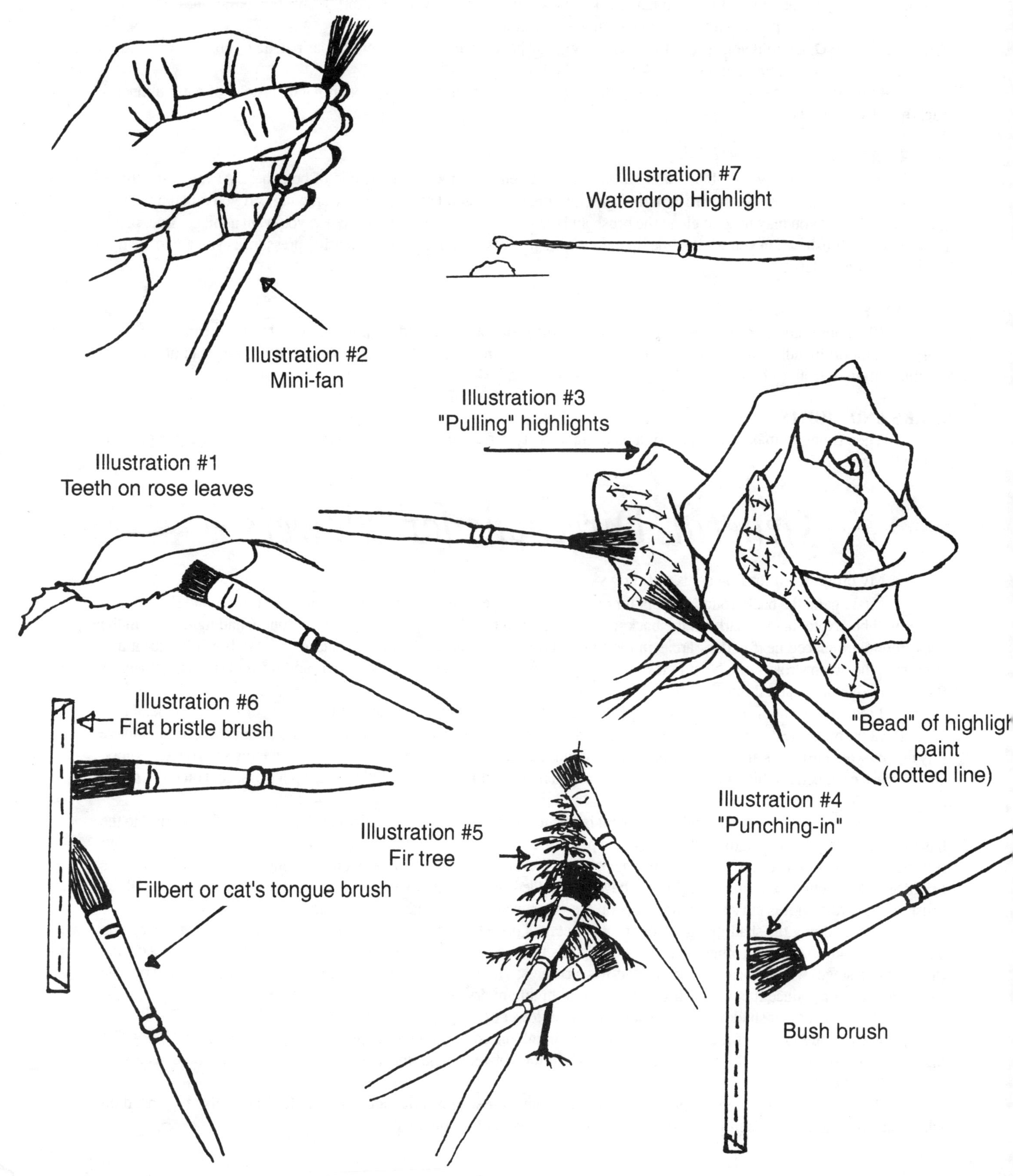

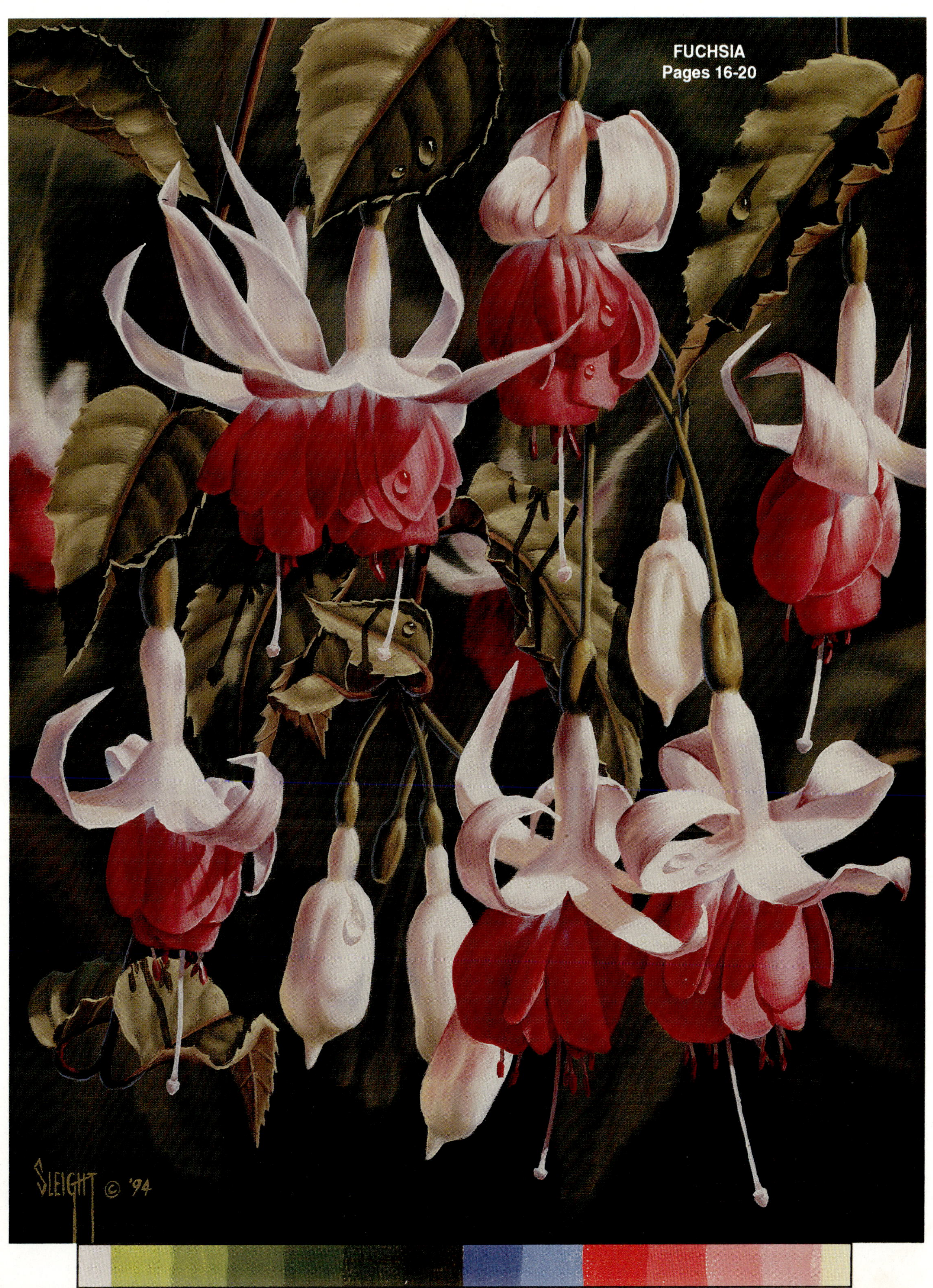
FUCHSIA
Pages 16-20
SLEIGHT © '94

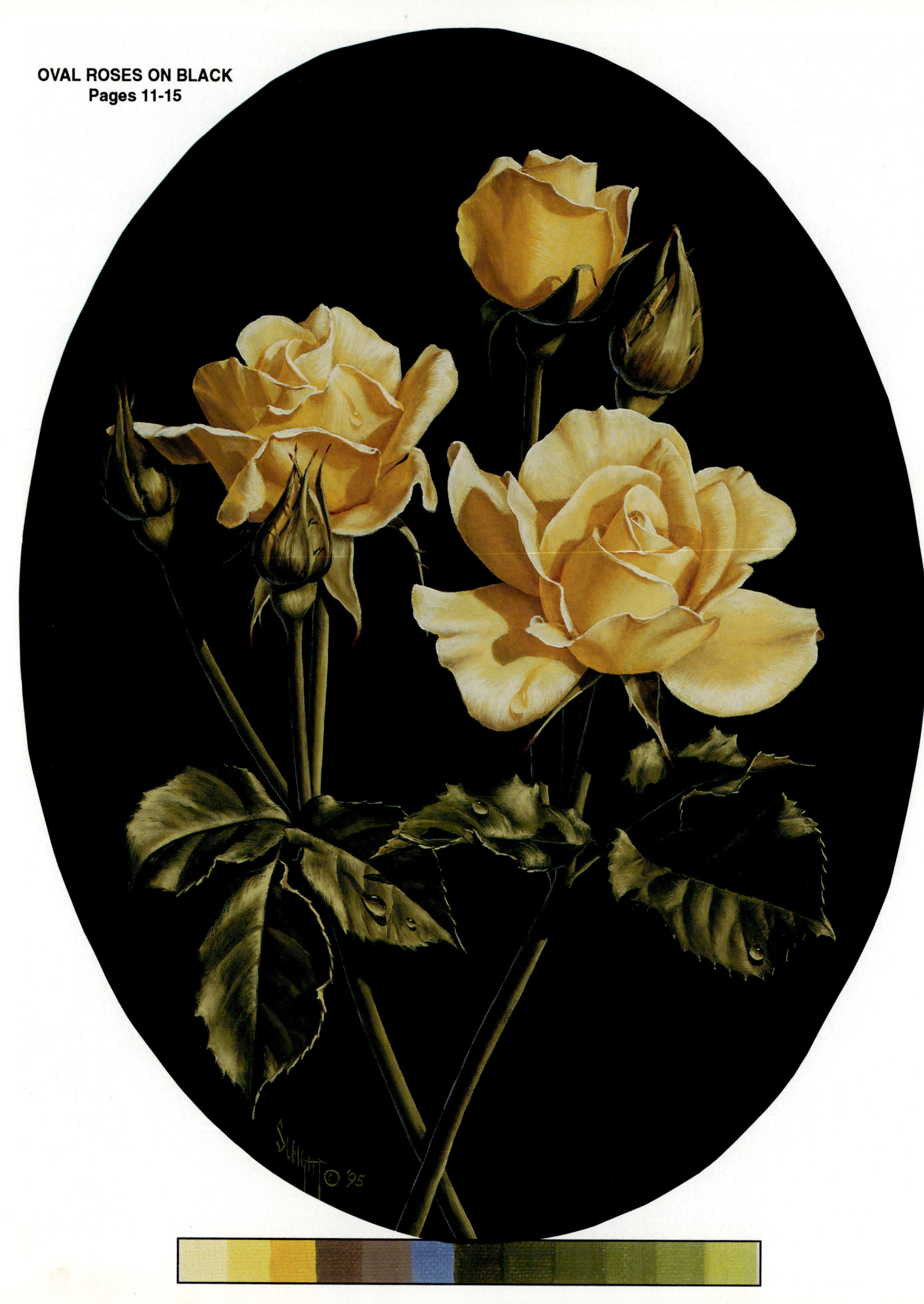

OVAL ROSES ON BLACK
Pages 11-15

# Oval Yellow Roses on Black

**CANVAS:** 11 X 14 Oval Black

## PALETTE

White
Cadmium Yellow Light (need very little)
Cadmium Yellow Medium
Cadmium Red Light
French Ultramarine Blue

Yellow Citron (Weber)
Leaf Green Medium (Weber)
Terre Verte (Weber)
Burnt Sienna

## BRUSHES

Mock Sable Liner - Preferably Long No. 4
Small Flat Mock Sables - No. 2 and No. 4 (or equivalent)
Mock Sable Cat's Tongue - No. 4
Small Bristle Fan Brush - No. 2 or No. 3
Optional - Small Round Mock Sable - No. 4
            No. 3 or No. 4 Sable Fan Brush

## MEDIUMS

Linseed Oil + Thinner or  Prepared Medium without drier
Liquin - (Winsor & Newton product)

**NOTE:** When working on black or grey canvases, always have a separate container of completely clean thinner to use only when cleaning paint off the background.

## MIX:

Highlight Yellow (1/8 tsp)............................ White + Cadmium Yellow Light
Light Yellow (1/2 tsp)................................. White + Cadmium Yellow Medium
Medium Yellow (1/4 tsp)............................. Light Yellow + more Cadmium Yellow Medium
Deep Lavender (1/4 tsp)............................. White + French Ultramarine Blue + Cadmium Red Light
Lavender (1/4 tsp).................................... Deep Lavender + White
Blue (1/8 tsp)........................................ White + French Ultramarine Blue
Dk. Green No. 1 (1/4 tsp)........................... Terre Verte + French Ultramarine Blue
*Dk. Green No. 2 (1/4 tsp)........................... Leaf Green Medium + French Ultramarine Blue
Med. Green No. 1 (1/4 tsp)........................... Dk. Green No. 2 + White + Yellow Citron
Med. Green No. 2 (1/4 tsp)........................... Med. Green No. 1 + White + Yellow Citron
Light Green (1/8 tsp)................................. Med. Green No. 2 + White + Yellow Citron
Highlight Green (1/8 tsp)............................. Light Green + White + Yellow Citron
*Make a large pile of this to start (1 tsp) so you can make the lighter green mixes from it

Transfer the pattern to the canvas using white transfer paper.  Use a soft eraser to remove any white that does not belong to the pattern.

## GREEN BUD

Start with the smaller flat mock sable brush, a <u>touch</u> of Liquin and dk. green No. 1 on the left side of the green bud on the left side of the canvas.  Change to dk. green No. 2, then med. green mixes as it gets lighter.  Paint light green mix in the lightest area and some extra Yellow Citron in the lower area just above the dark shade.  Brush lightly with your small fan brush (sable or bristle) to straighten out the brush strokes and blend a little.  Be sure not to brush over the edges into the black background.  If you do get any color in the background, remove immediately with the clean thinner.

Let this dry a little while you put a "base" coat on the left yellow rose (see below).  When the paint on the bud has become slightly sticky instead of slippery, reinforce the dark areas with more dk. green No. 1 using a cat's tongue or a liner brush (no medium).  Add some Burnt Sienna in some areas with the cat's tongue brush.  Soften again with the corner of the small fan brush.  Add some Burnt Sienna to the tips of the bud using a liner brush and thinner.

## Oval Yellow Roses on Black continued
### GREEN BUD continued

Mix a softened pile of the highlight green as described at the end of the instructions. Place a line of this across the highlighted areas; then stroke over it in a curved, downward direction with your liner brush made into a mini-fan (see instructions at end of text). Turn painting upside down and stroke across the highlight in the opposite direction. Clean and dry the brush, then pull at the ends of the highlights to blend them in a little (this is very hard to do if the base coat is dry, so try to do it while the paint is at least a little wet).

Use the blue mix, a liner brush and thinner to put a backlight on the lower left side of the bud and stem. (Stem is painted with dk. green No. 1 on the left side, dk. green No. 2 on right where stem is in shadow, light green mix where it is not in shadow. Blend colors lightly with liner brush or cat's tongue).

### YELLOW ROSE ON LEFT

Starting on the left side with the smaller mock sable brush, use the light yellow mix in the lightest areas, medium yellow mix in the slightly darker areas (that are not in shadow) and Cadmium Yellow Medium in the shadow areas. Block in only three or four petals at a time. Use little or no Liquin with the lt. yellow mix. It is okay to use it with the Cadmium Yellow Medium. Leave small cracks where the lines are until you have done enough shading to separate the petals. Leave cracks also where the highlighted edges of petals are until the highlights are added.

With the cat's tongue brush, blend lavender mix into the shadows, and dk. green No. 2 into the underside of the petal hanging over the green bud. Soften these a little with the corner of the small fan brush. If the brush leaves "scratch" marks, try using a sable fan or the mini-fan made from your liner brush.

Let this dry a little while you finish the green bud.

Before adding more shading, etc. to the flower, put a base coat on more petals.

On the first petals, use the cat's tongue brush to reinforce the dark color using more Cadmium Yellow Medium and the deep lavender mix. Add a touch of Cadmium Red light and/or Burnt Sienna where necessary to "warm" it up. Add more light and medium yellow mixes where needed to cover the black background more completely. This covers better if you use a cat's tongue brush to put it on (no Liquin).

Soften each petal again with a fan brush, or the mini-fan in small places. Add a few more dark accents with your liner brush and Burnt Sienna, especially just above the bottom right petal. If you've lost the small crack between the two right hand petals, try using a small chisel edged brush and a little thinner to clean it off. If this doesn't work, wait until it is dry and paint some black over the spot.

Put a base coat on the rest of the petals on this flower as before so it can be drying some while you work on the upper yellow bud and the highlights on the first petals.

### UPPER YELLOW BUD

Block in this bud in the same way you did the first one, only keep this one a little darker yellow-not so much light mix. Do a little shading with Cadmium Yellow Medium and the lavender mix (cat's tongue brush) and brush it lightly with fan as before.

After putting the highlight on the flower on the left (see below), go back and finish this bud in the same way (add more shading and dark colors, brush with the fan brush and highlight).

### HIGHLIGHTS ON FIRST FLOWER

Make a softened pile of some of the highlight yellow. Add highlights along the tops of some petals with your liner brush. Note that the thickness or width of this "line" varies quite a bit. If you get it too thick in some places, come up under it with the shadow color on your liner brush. Where the highlight is more blended, lay a "bead" of highlight yellow along the area and then brush over it very lightly as before with your mini-fan, first in one direction, then in the opposite direction. Turn painting upside down or sideways if necessary.

**NOTE:** The thickness of the bead of paint that you lay down in these areas depends on how far you have to stretch it - if the area to be highlighted is large, you'll need a thicker line than in smaller areas.

Highlights within shadow areas are Cadmium Yellow Light + Cadmium Yellow Medium - use liner brush and thinner.

Paint the calyxes (green part) on the left flower with the green mixes, adding a touch of Burnt Sienna (not enough to turn it brown). Use dk. green No. 1 on the left calyx; highlight it with med. green No. 1 + the blue mix + a touch of French Ultramarine Blue. Highlight the other calyxes with a lighter shade of the highlight green (add White) + a touch of Burnt Sienna.

### BUDS

Paint the other two green buds the same way as the first one. Use medium yellow mix in the areas where a petal shows and shade those areas with Cadmium Yellow Medium + lavender mix.

## Oval Yellow Roses on Black continued
### RIGHT SIDE FLOWER
Paint this flower in the same way as the left rose.

### STEMS
Use dark green No. 1 down the left side and all the way across where the stems are in shadow.  Paint medium green No. 2 down the right side elsewhere.  (Use smaller flat mock sable brush with a good chisel edge and Liquin).  Put dk. green No. 2 down the middle, then blend with dry cat's tongue brush, stroking lengthwise down the stems.  Let them dry a <u>little</u>.

Highlight the right side (except in shadow areas) with a liner brush, thinner and the highlight green.  Blend into the stem with a dry liner brush.  Backlight with the blue mix along the left side in the same way as the highlight.  Make sure the backlight color is dark enough that it doesn't look like a highlight.  Add a little Burnt Sienna down the middle of some stems with your cat's tongue brush (no Liquin).

### LEAVES
Using a flat mock sable brush and Liquin, fill in the lightest areas of the leaves (one or two leaves at a time) with light green, middle tone areas with medium greens, darker areas with dk. green No. 2, and darkest shadows with dk. green No. 1.  Don't try to do a lot of detail yet, just put in the colors.  Use the corner of the chisel edge brush to form the teeth along the edges.  Note that some edges are darker than the color next to them-use a smaller brush there.

Use the cat's tongue brush to put the shading in along the vein lines, generally using one shade darker in the lighter areas, one shade lighter in the darkest areas.  The leaves will not be as bright yet as the final ones - highlights will be added later.  Brush lightly with your fan brush either from the center-line out to the edge or from the edge in towards the center, being careful not to brush over the outside edges.  Let this dry awhile (NOTE - the greens will dry much faster than the lighter yellow shades, so don't wait too long).

When the paint is sticky, reinforce the darks using a liner brush if necessary.  Use a liner brush and the softened pile of highlight green (mixed for the green buds) to put a line along the highlighted areas (don't get it too thick).  Make a mini-fan out of your liner brush and stroke over the lines to spread out the highlight.  Where the highlight is along the edge, use less paint (and a touch of thinner if necessary).

### THORNS
This particular rose (called Sun Flare) has no thorns.  If you want to add some anyway, use your liner brush, thinner and Burnt Sienna.  Blend the base of them slightly into the stem.  Highlight with White + Burnt Sienna.

### WATERDROPS
Follow directions in front of book.  Be careful not to get the colors too dark.  On the flowers, use medium yellow mix + lavender or deep lavender mix for the dark shade, highlight yellow for the light shade.

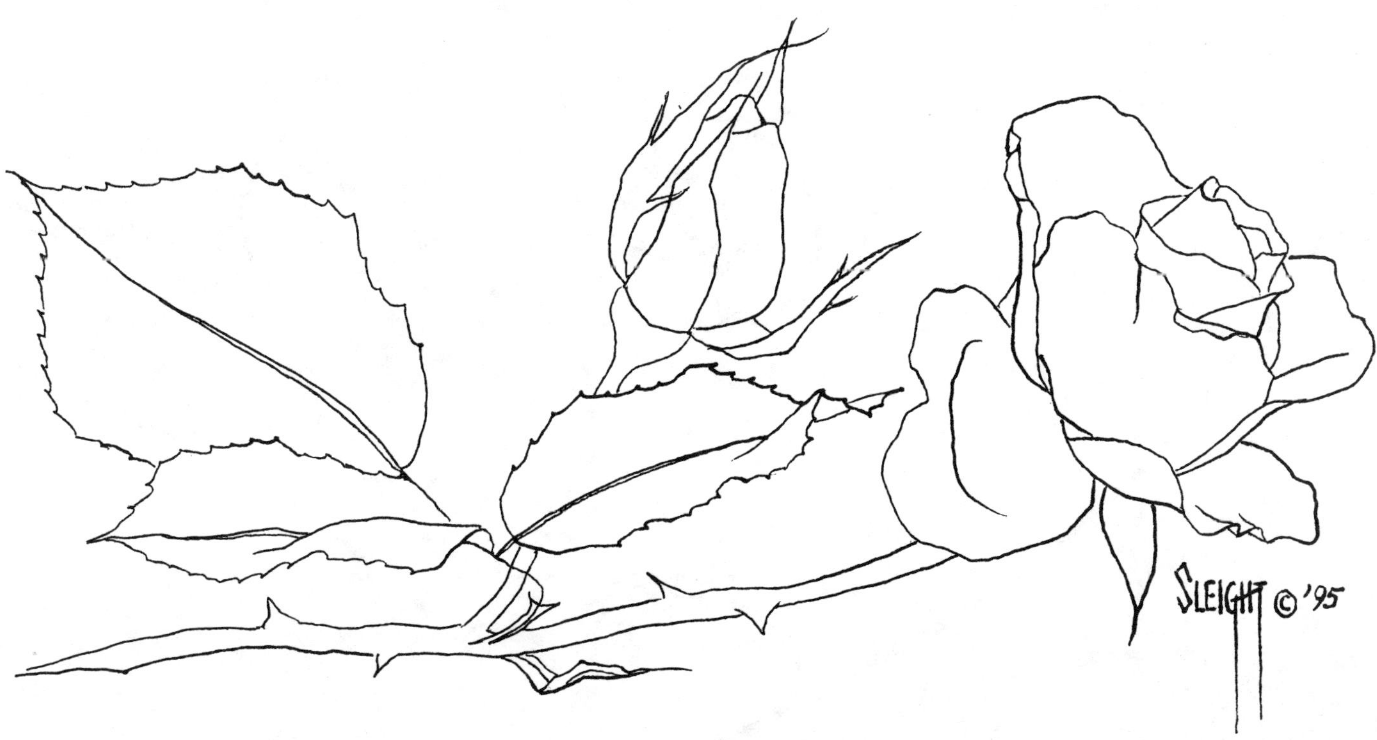

# OVAL YELLOW ROSES

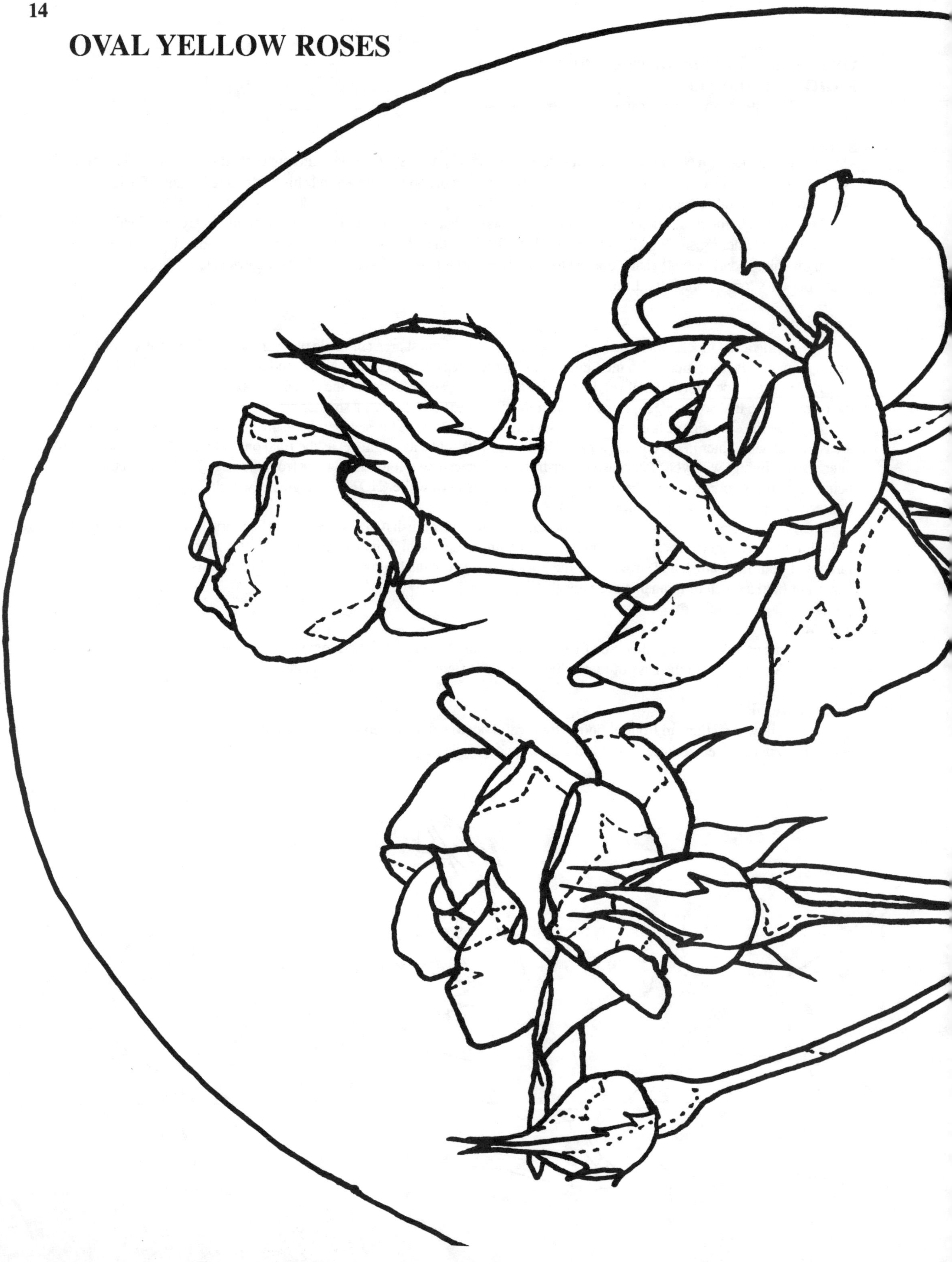

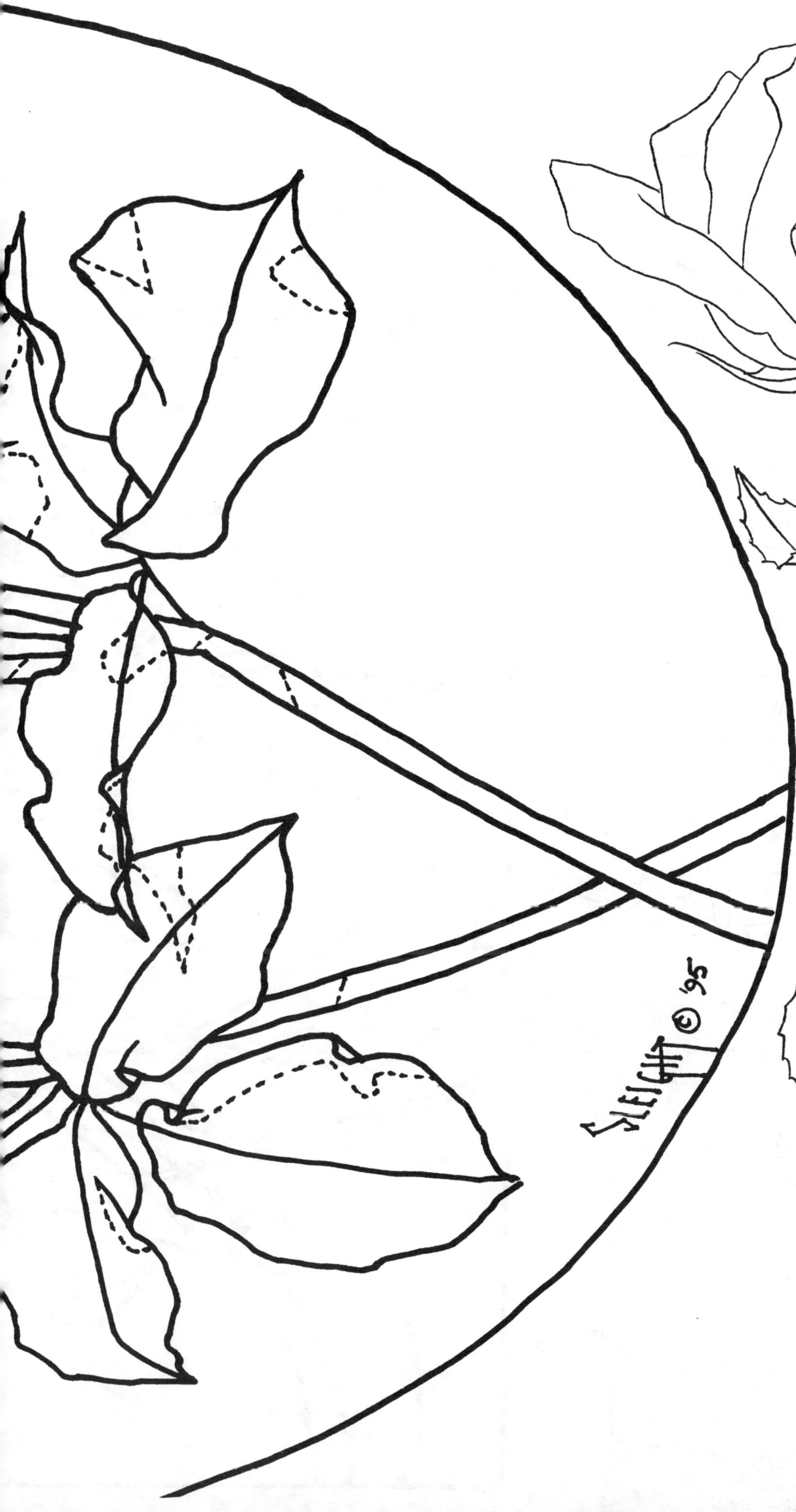

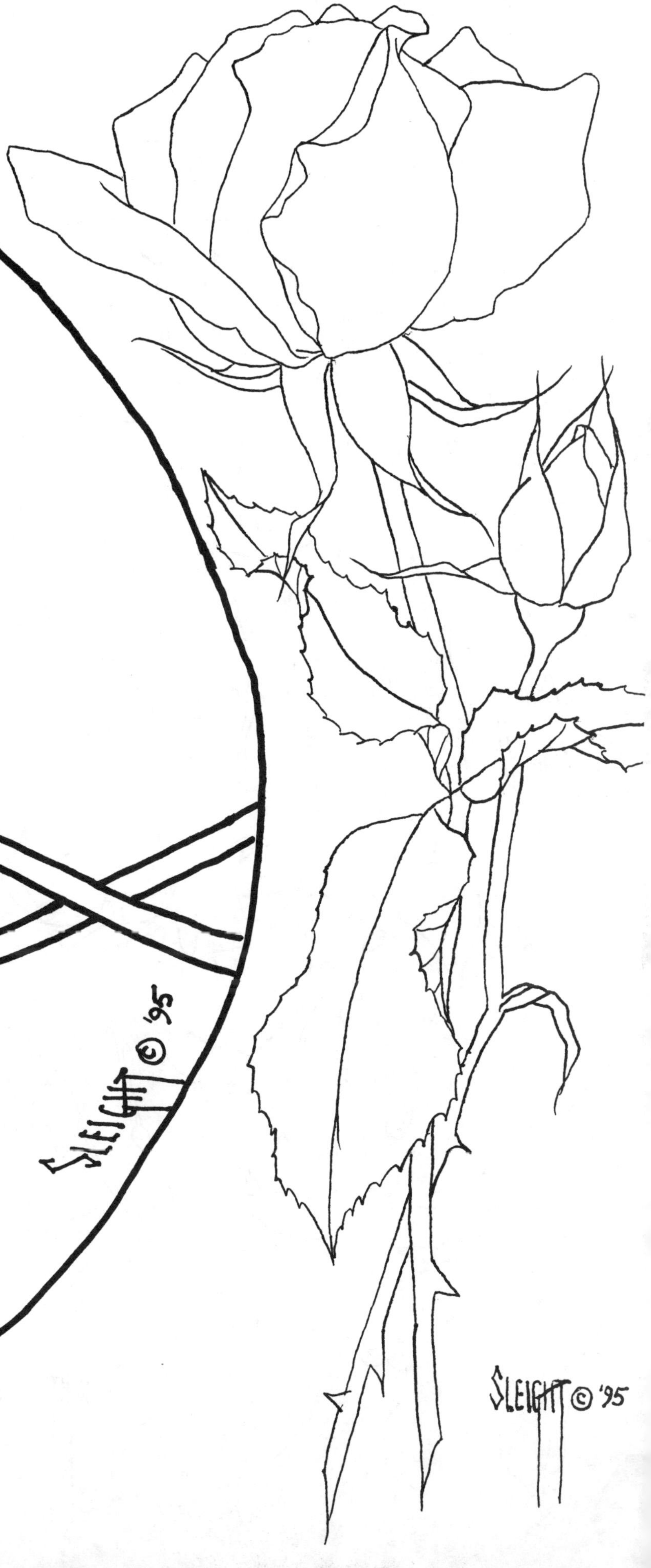

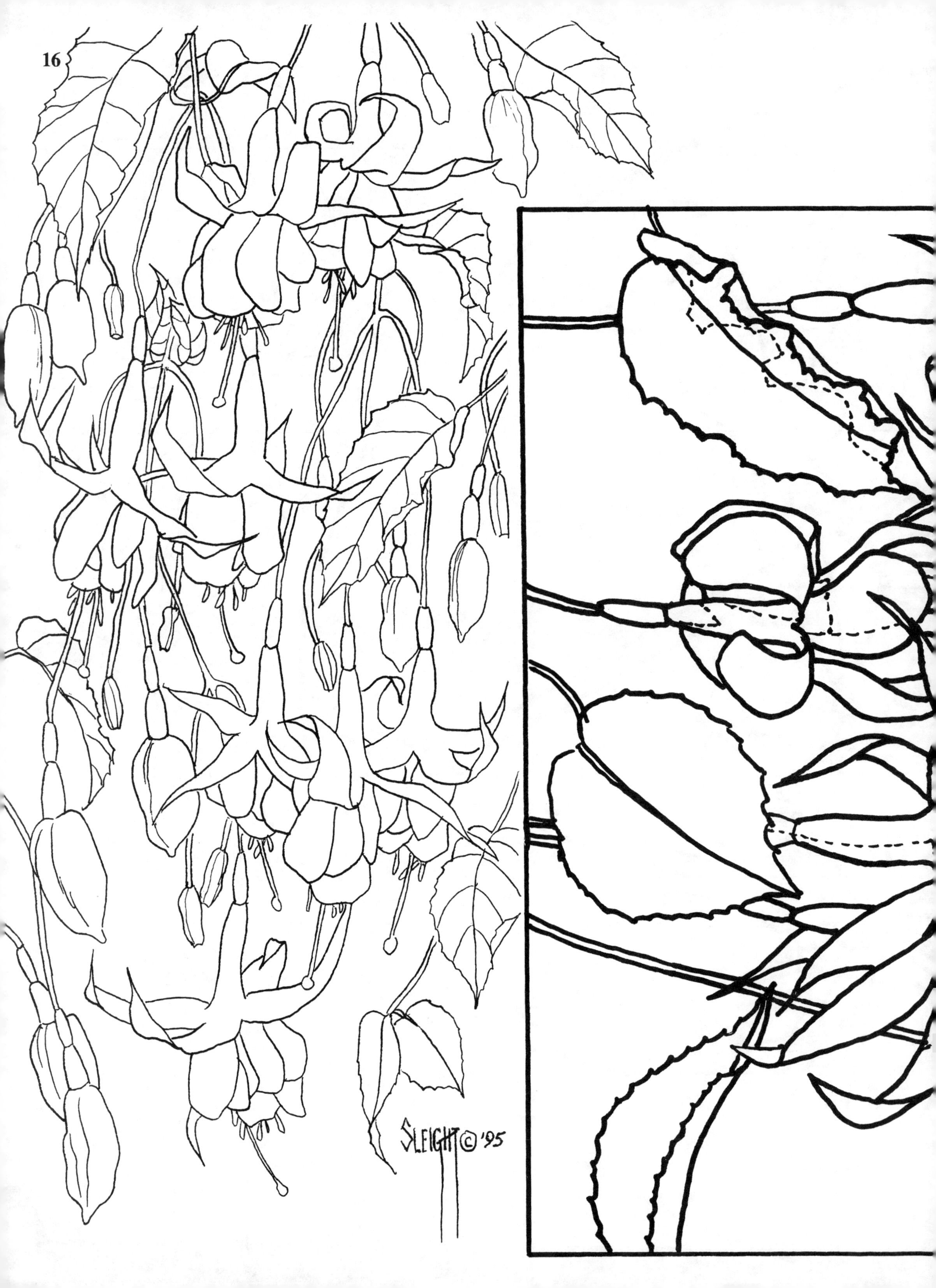

SLEIGHT © '95

*My sons gave me a hanging basket of these beautiful flowers for Mother's day and they served as my inspiration for this painting.*

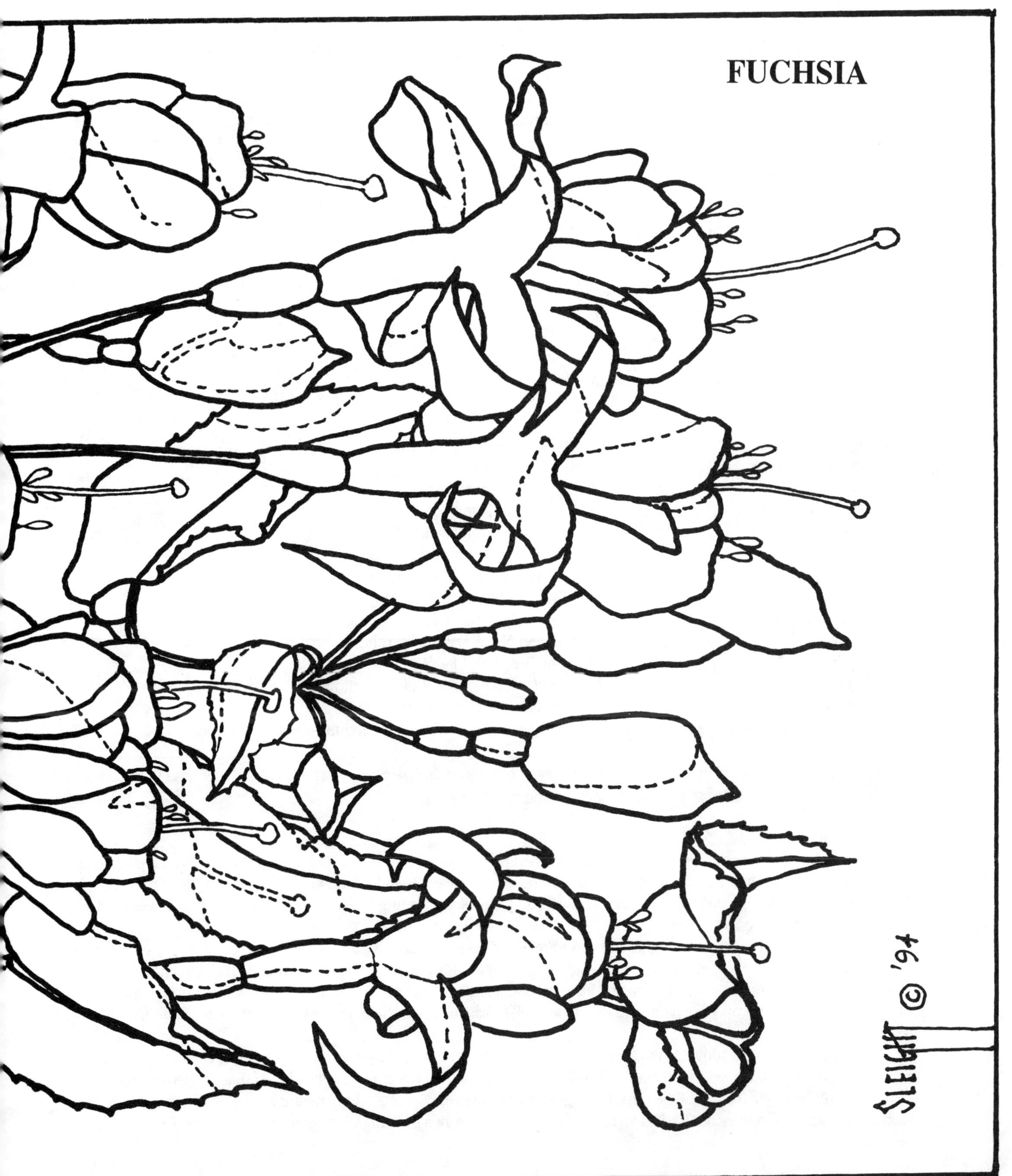

# *Fuchsia*

**CANVAS:** 9 x 12 White

**PALETTE**

| | |
|---|---|
| White | Yellow Citron (Weber) |
| Cadmium Yellow Light | Leaf Green Medium (Weber) |
| Cadmium Red Light | Terre Verte (Weber) |
| Grumbacher Red | Burnt Sienna |
| Alizarin Crimson | Burnt Umber |
| French Ultramarine Blue | |

**BRUSHES**

Liners - Preferably Long No. 4
Flat Mock Sables - No. 2 and No. 4 (or equivalent)
Mock Sable Cat's Tongue - No. 4
Small Bristle Fan Brush - No. 2 or No. 3
Flat or Filbert Bristle Brush - No. 4 or No. 5 and No. 2 or No. 3

**MEDIUMS**

Liquin (Winsor & Newton)
Linseed Oil + Thinner (or prepared medium WITHOUT a drier)

**MIX:**

Cream (1/4 tsp)..............................................White + Cadmium Yellow Light
Highlight Pink (1/8 tsp)................................White + Grumbacher Red
Light Pink (1/8 tsp)....................................... White + more Grumbacher Red
Medium Pink (1/8 tsp)................................... White + more Grumbacher Red
Deep Pink (1/8 tsp)....................................... White + more Grumbacher Red
Light Blue (1/8 tsp)....................................... White + French Ultramarine Blue
Medium Blue (1/8 tsp)................................... White + more French Ultramarine Blue
Dark Green No. 1 (1/4 tsp)............................Terre Verte + French Ultramarine Blue
*Dark Green No. 2 (1/4 tsp).........................Leaf Green Medium + French Ultramarine Blue
Medium Green No. 1 (1/4 tsp)......................Dark Green No. 2 + White + Yellow Citron
Medium Green No. 2 (1/4 tsp)......................Medium Green No. 1 + White + Yellow Citron
Light Green (1/8 tsp).....................................Medium Green No. 2 + White + Yellow Citron
Highlight Green (1/8 tsp)..............................Light Green + White + Yellow Citron

*Make a larger pile of this to start (about 1 tsp.) so you can make the lighter green mixes from it.

Transfer the pattern to your canvas using grey or black graphite paper. Try to keep the shadow lines (dashed lines) in the white areas of the <u>flowers very light (erase a little if necessary).</u>

**BACKGROUND**

Start at the top with a No. 4 or No. 5 flat or filbert bristle brush, Liquin, and medium green No. 2 mixed with some medium blue in the lighter areas, dark green No. 1 in the darker areas. Blend a little medium blue into the dark green No. 1 in a few places. Paint around the foreground flowers and leaves, continuing to add some medium blue in places until you get down to the background flowers.

Pay attention to where the lights and darks are as these are planned to show off the foreground flowers and leaves. Don't worry about the background stems yet and come in real close to the foreground stems. It's better to cover them completely than to leave too large a space and have to have a really fat stem!! Also, paint right over the foreground stamen - it's easier to paint them over dry paint. Change to a smaller bristle brush where necessary. Keep the paint smooth, but not too thin.

Stop when you get down to the background flowers. Put the upper petals of these in with the cream mix and a little Liquin. Don't shade them yet - let them dry a little first. Don't put the lower (red) petals in yet, but leave room for them.

Paint on down the rest of the canvas using all but the highlight green, a little medium blue mix here and there, and working a touch of Grumbacher Red into a few places. You can work a little highlight green over the darker green colors if necessary.

## Fuchsia continued
### BACKGROUND continued

The lowest part of the canvas is almost entirely dark green No. 1. The up-turned part of the leaf midway down the right side is painted with cream + Burnt Sienna + light green mix.

Shade the top petals of the background flowers with the medium pink + medium blue and a touch of Cadmium Yellow Light. It should be a bit more yellow on the left side. Brush mix a little of these colors on your palette. Blend them into the shadow areas on the petals, then balance the shade by adding more medium blue or medium or light pink (a touch of Cadmium Yellow Light greys the mix slightly).

Use a good chisel edge brush to make the background stems using medium green No. 2 for the green ones, Burnt Sienna and then White + Burnt Sienna for the brown ones. Brush each stem lengthwise lightly with the corner of the fan brush, then lightly brush everything horizontally again over the whole canvas.

Using the small fan brush, blue out the background using an "X" stroke over it very lightly, then horizontal strokes across the entire canvas. If the paint streaks a lot, it's either too wet or you have too much paint on. Skim some paint off with your palette knife or wait for it to dry a little longer. The background should be blurred enough that there are no sharp edges remaining.

Paint the lower (red) petals in the background with Grumbacher Red in the darker areas, light pink in the lighter areas. Darken the shadow areas with Alizarin Crimson, then Alizarin Crimson + dark green No. 1. A cat's tongue brush works well for this. Let this dry a bit while you start on some of the upper leaves in the foreground.

When the red is getting a little sticky (test with your cat's tongue brush), use the corner of the fan brush to blend within each petal, then around the edges to blue them. Finish by brushing very lightly across the whole flower. If it streaks too much, wait awhile and try again. Be sure to have these background flowers done before you paint the foreground leaves or flowers near them.

**NOTE:** If you must stop painting before the background is completed, be sure to fan brush the part that you have done. Once it is dry, it cannot be blurred!

Use the chisel edge of the larger flat mock sable brush and thinner to clean paint off the foreground flowers and leaves. Refer to your pattern if you've lost your lines.

### LEAVES

Use the larger flat mock sable brush, Liquin and any of the greens except the highlight green. (Use the smaller flat brush for smaller areas). Paint the shade of green that is dominant in each area of the leaf, not the darkest or the lightest. Blend darker or lighter green shades into this as necessary. Add a touch of Burnt Sienna to the lighter greens for the underside of the leaves where they show. Don't try to get the brightest areas as light as the finished ones are yet. You will add highlights later.

The shadows on the leaves are dark green No. 1. The shadows cast on the leaves from the flowers and stamen can be painted on after the painting is dry. Use some Liquin in your paint for this so it is slightly transparent (this is called "glazing").

Form the "teeth" along the edges of the leaves the same way as you would for the leaves on roses (see illustrations in front of book). Use the corner of a good chisel edge flat brush (either of the flat mock sable brushes).

Use the No. 4 cat's tongue brush to put the vein areas on each side using the next darker shade of green. You may need to let the basecoat dry a little before doing this. Then brush each side with the fan brush either from the center out or from the edge towards the center. Brush down toward the tip to soften the "striped" look, then out from the center again.

Put the vein down the center of the leaves with light green + Burnt Sienna, a liner brush and thinner. This should get skinnier as it approaches the tip of the leaf.

Make a softened pile of some of the highlight green (see definitions in front of the book). With a liner brush, put a line of this paint along an area to be highlighted. How thick the line is should be determined by how big the area is to be highlighted. Form a mini-fan out of your long liner (see definitions) and use it to spread out the highlight. Brush across the line of paint very lightly in a slight curve. Turn the painting upside down or sideways and brush across the line in the opposite direction. If the highlight is very close to the center vein, just barely pull at the inside of the line, but don't get it too close to the vein. Where only the edge of the leaf is highlighted, thin down some of the highlight green and use a liner brush (but don't blend it at all).

The brown stems are painted with Burnt Umber, liner brush and thinner on the left (shadow) side, light green + Burnt Sienna on the right. Blend these two together in the middle. Keep the stems thin to start with as they do tend to "grow". Where the stems are in shadow, they are entirely Burnt Umber. Put a backlight on the left side with the medium blue mix and a touch more French Ultramarine Blue and thinner. Blend this slightly into the Burnt Umber.

## Fuchsia continued
### FLOWERS

Paint the top petals with the cream mix, a touch of Liquin and the smaller flat mock sable brush. Let this dry awhile before shading them.

Paint in the blue area between the top and bottom petals with the lt. blue mix. Make this area larger than it appears on the final picture.

While this is drying a little, you could put a "base coat" on some more leaves.

When the cream color on the top petals has dried enough, shade them with med. blue + lt. or med. pink, and a touch of Cadmium Yellow Light where the color appears warmer. The cat's tongue brush works especially well here - except along an edge where you may want to use the smaller flat mock sable brush.

Soften each petal very carefully with the corner of your fan brush. Add some white to some of the cream mix, then make a softened pile as you did with the highlight green. Use a liner brush to add this to the petals. It goes mostly along the edges (but not all edges), but also within some of the petals where there is a curve or bend in the petal. Brush across these with the mini-fan as you did on the leaves.

Paint Grumbacher Red and a touch of Liquin into the petals where they are red (not pink). Use the flat mock sable brushes. You should be able to go right over your lines and still see them. If not, leave little cracks where the lines are until you get some shading in. Don't blend into the blue yet - just go up to it. When both the blue shade and the red are a little drier, blend them together _slightly_ using the side of the cat's tongue brush and stroking very lightly. Wipe the brush between _every_ stroke.

Where the petals are pink, use the light or medium pink mixes, and shadow with the deep pink and/or Grumbacher Red (a cat's tongue brush works great for this). Shadow the red areas with Alizarin Crimson. You probably will find that the Alizarin won't show much at first. Wait awhile and try again when it's a little drier. You may even need to wait overnight (the reds are very slow drying colors).

For the darkest shadows, add some dk. green #1 to some Alizarin Crimson. The highlights within the shadow areas are Cadmium Red Light (add a touch of thinner). Brush each petal lightly with the corner of the fan brush to straighten the brush strokes out and blend a little (be careful not to brush over the edges of the petals). Highlight the pink areas with a softened pile of highlight pink. These petals don't need very intense highlights.

Paint the green stems with dk. green No. 1 on the left side, and lt. green on the right, blending the two together down the middle. Backlight them with a darker shade of med. blue as with the brown stems. Add a little Yellow Citron to the green part between the flower and the stem. Highlight the upper right of this with the highlight green.

### BUDS

Start with the cream mix. Shade with med. pink + med. blue and a touch of Cadmium Yellow Light as you did with the tops of the flowers. Keep the left side more pale yellow with a touch of lt. pink added (add a little more Cadmium Yellow Light to some cream mix, then a touch of light pink). Shade the bottom of the three lowest buds with med. green No. 1 and/or No. 2.

### STAMEN

These are easiest to do when the painting is completely dry. Paint the "white" ones with the cream mix, liner brush and thinner. Shadow them with the same color as on the upper petals, but with a little more Cadmium Yellow Light and blue added. Highlight with the highlight color from the upper petals.

The red stamen are painted with Grumbacher Red (and thinner) first; then shadow with Alizarin Crimson. Highlight where necessary with the deep pink mix.

### WATERDROPS

Follow directions in front of the book. Be careful not to get the colors too dark. On the leaves the dark color is dk. green No. 2 and/or No. 1.

On the flowers, use Grumbacher Red for the dark, adding a little Alizarin Crimson to the shadow only. Use the light pink mix for the light color.

For the white petals, mix a color similar to your shadow tones, only a little lighter (lt. pink + lt. blue) and a little greyer (add more Cadmium Yellow Light). Don't get this too pink.

SLEIGHT © '95

# White Roses

**CANVAS:** 11 x 14 White

**PALETTE**

White
Cadmium Yellow Light
Cadmium Yellow Medium
Raw Sienna
Grumbacher Red (just a touch)

French Ultramarine Blue
Yellow Citron (Weber)
Leaf Green Medium (Weber)
Terre Verte (Weber)
Burnt Sienna

**BRUSHES**

Filbert Bristle - No. 6
Flat Bristle - No. 2
Flat Mock Sables - No. 2 and No. 4 (or equivalent)
Mock Sable Cat's Tongue - No. 4
Liner - preferably long No. 4
Small Bristle Fan Brush - No. 2 or No. 3
No. 1 Mop or other Blender Brush (not too big)

**MEDIUM**

Liquin (Winsor & Newton)
Linseed Oil + Thinner

**MIX:**

White Mix (1/8 tsp)......................................White + touch of Cadmium Yellow Light
Cream (1/2 tsp)............................................White + Cadmium Yellow Medium + touch Grumbacher Red
Lt. Blue (1/2 tsp).........................................White + French Ultramarine Blue + touch Raw Sienna
Med. Blue (1/4 tsp).....................................White + more French Ultramarine Blue + more Raw Sienna
Greyed Blue (1/4 tsp)..................................Med. blue + French Ultramarine Blue + Raw Sienna + touch
Grumbacher Red
Dk. Green No. 1 (1/2 tsp)............................Terre Verte + French Ultramarine Blue
*Dk. Green No. 2 (1/4 tsp)...........................Leaf Green Med. + French Ultramarine Blue
Med. Green No. 1 (1/2 tsp)..........................Dk Green No. 2 + White + Yellow Citron
Med. Green No. 2 (1/2 tsp)..........................Med. Green No. 1 + White + Yellow Citron
Highlight Green (1/4 tsp).............................Med. Green No. 2 + White + Yellow Citron

*Make a larger amount of this mix (about 1 tsp) to start so you can make the lighter green mixes from it.

After transferring the pattern to your canvas (using graphite paper), lightly sketch the background buds and flowers in with a small brush, Raw Sienna and thinner.

**BACKGROUND**

Start in the upper right corner with the lt. blue mix and the No. 6 filbert bristle brush. Scrub the paint on using the side of the bristles. Try to avoid using any medium if possible, but if you must, use the linseed oil + thinner mixture, not Liquin. Bring this color all the way across the top of the canvas, about 4-1/2 inches down the right side, and about 2-1/2 inches down the left side. Stay a little bit away from the upper flower, and leave some space for the background bud.

Overlap this with a mixture of med. blue + dk. green No. 1 (more blue than green). Suggest some leaf shapes, but leave most strokes loose - don't overblend. Gradually add more dk. green No. 1 to the mixture as you work down around the upper flower and towards the left side.

By the time you get about midway down the larger bloom (on right) and to the left of the flower on the left, you should use only dk. green No. 1 - no blue mix. You can also start using some of the lighter green mixes and a little Burnt Sienna. Don't use any highlight green mix unless you blend it well into the other colors.

At some point, stop and go back above and add some lighter greens into the top area. Blend these in well - they should not be too light.

Paint the upper <u>background</u> bud using the cream mix+ Cadmium Yellow Medium, where the flower color is, and the green mixes for the calyxes (see definitions in front of book). Paint the ends of the calyxes out over the background, adding a little Burnt Sienna at the tips (use liner brush for this).

## White Roses continued
### BACKGROUND continued

Paint in the lower background bud and the background flower (lower right) before you put the greens in around them. Start with the cream mix and a little Liquin. Shade the bud with a little Cadmium Yellow Medium and the greyed blue mix, then put the green calyxes around it. Shade the flower with Cadmium Yellow Medium, the greyed blue mix and some Raw Sienna. Let this dry some while you finish the rest of the background. Come back later and add more greyed blue mix into the flower if necessary. Extend the tips of the calyxes on the bud after the background has been put in around it.

In the rest of the background, you can paint in the more distant background leaves first and then paint around them, or put them in when you get down to them.

The lighter reddish brown color in the background is Burnt Sienna with one or both of the med. green mixes added (mix on the canvas). The darker color at the bottom is Burnt Sienna + dk. green No. 1.

Repeat any shading or highlighting needed in the more distinct background leaves where necessary for definition.

Using a blender brush (mop brush or fan brush - not too big), brush lightly over the background colors to blur them starting in the upper right corner. Be careful not to drag the green colors back over the blue area - wipe the brush well on a rag periodically. Do not clean your brush in thinner unless absolutely necessary (the thinner will take paint off the background), but if you must, be sure to dry it as well as you can. See (*) for solutions to other problems.

I use a crisscross stroke over most of the background. You may find it helpful to first brush within and around the edges of the flower, buds and more distinct leaves (use just the corner of the fan brush where necessary). Then go over them lightly with crisscross strokes. Finish with horizontal strokes over the entire canvas.

*If the paint streaks too much, wait until it is a little drier. Another reason it may streak is too much paint. If this is the case, skim (don't scrape) your palette knife across the canvas to remove excess paint; then try brushing again.

*If the paint is too dry, it won't blur. Try using a stiffer fan brush to blend. If necessary, wet the brush with just a touch of thinner. If the paint is completely dry it is impossible to blur it, even adding medium, so try very hard to get it brushed out before it dries. NOTE - the nylon canvas dries faster so you may need to stop part way down and brush the upper part before continuing.

Another reason the paint might not blur, is not enough paint. If this is the case, simply add more paint in those areas.

Clean off any paint that has streaked over the foreground flowers and leaves using a flat mock sable brush and thinner. Refer to your pattern if necessary for lost lines.

### FLOWER ON LEFT

Put a base coat on the entire bud with the cream mix and Liquin. Use the No. 2 and No. 4 flat mock sable brushes. If you can't see your lines through the paint, leave cracks where they are, or do a little shading as you proceed (with the greyed blue mix). Add a touch of Cadmium Yellow Medium to a corner of the cream mix with your brush, then apply this in the yellower areas. Some areas are very delicate - don't use too much Cadmium Yellow Medium.

Work more greyed blue mix into the darker areas. Some med. blue mix is also used in some of the shadows (look for the "bluer" areas). For the darkest shadows (two petals on left and shadow on front petal), add a little more French Ultramarine Blue and Raw Sienna to some of the greyed blue mix (with your brush). If you can't get the shadows dark enough, let it dry awhile and then try again.

Add a little dk. green No. 1 and No. 2 into the underside of the front petal (just above the calyx). Blend a touch of Raw Sienna and more greyed blue into the lower left area of the left petal (just above the left calyx).

Brush each petal with the small fan brush to smooth the paint out, brushing in the direction the petal is curving. Where there is a cast shadow (hard edge instead of soft edge), don't brush over the shadow edge. Brush up to it and then on the other side of it. Be sure not to brush over the edges of the petals themselves either.

**NOTE:** This bud won't appear as bright at this stage as the final picture - highlights will be added later.

Fill in the calyxes below the left flower with dk. green No. 1 and Liquin. Use this color also for the upper (darker) part of the stem. Add a touch of Burnt Sienna to the tips of the calyxes with a liner brush and thinner.

### UPPER FLOWER

Let this dry a little, while you put a base coat on the upper flower using the same mixtures as before. On the left side of the left petal, use the darkened version of the greyed blue mix and then some dk. green No. 1. Brush each petal with the fan brush as before.

Use the med. green mixes and some dk. green No. 1 for the lighter calyx on the left side.

While this bud dries a little, go back and put highlights on the first one.

## White Roses continued
### HIGHLIGHTS

Make a softened pile (see definitions in front of book) of some of the white mix. Use your liner brush to apply this. Along the top of some petals, it remains a line. Where you want a thicker line, press a little harder with the brush (also load more paint onto the brush). On a curving petal, place a bead of paint along the crest of the curve-usually in from the edge. The size of the petal dictates the thickness of the line (smaller petal - less paint).

Clean the brush; then make a mini-fan out of your liner. Brush lightly across the bead of paint in a curve. Turn the paint upside down (or sideways) and continue the curve in the opposite direction.

**"Highlights" on Calyxes":**  Add some French Ultramarine Blue to some med. green No. 1. Using your liner brush and thinner, put this color along the edges of the calyx. Make a rather thick line across the "bend" area of the two calyxes on the right and pull across it with the mini-fan as before.

### STEMS

Paint dk. green No. 1 down the left side of the stems, dk. green No. 2 down the middle, med. green No. 2 down the right side. Blend, brushing up and down the stem with a small cat's tongue brush or a small round brush. Add a backlight along the left side of the entire stem with the med. blue mix + more French Ultramarine Blue (liner brush and thinner), blending slightly into the green.

Make a softened pile of some of the highlight green and add to the right side of the stem, brushing lightly into the stem colors.

### FULL BLOOM

Paint this flower as you did the other two. If you don't have enough time to finish the whole flower before it dries, just put a base coat on what you think you can finish.

Add Cadmium Yellow Medium, Raw Sienna and a darkened greyed blue mix in the darkest "gold" areas.

For the dark area on the lower left petal (just below the middle petal), first use the greyed blue and blue mixes on the entire shadow; then Cadmium Yellow Medium, then dk green No. 1 leaving some of the previous color showing each time. If you have trouble getting it dark enough, let it dry awhile, then try again.

Where there is a highlight within a shadow area, mix some cream mix + Cadmium Yellow Medium + a touch of greyed blue. Be sure it's not too light. Apply this in the same way as the previous highlights, but not quite as thick.

### LEAVES

Put a base coat on the three leaves on the left using the green mix that is dominant in each area ( use dk. green No. 1 where it is darkest, then dk. green No. 2, then the med. green mixes). Don't put the "stripes" or veins in yet, or the highlight green. Use the corner of one of the flat mock sable brushes to form the teeth along the edge of the leaves. Where the teeth are highlighted, put them in with the darker color next to them first and highlight later.

Brush the leaves with your fan brush, brushing from the center out, or from the edge towards the center (be careful not to brush across the outside edge).

Add the veins with a smaller brush - cat's tongue or small round brush and darker color (dk. green No. 1 or No. 2). If the base coat is too wet, wait awhile and try again. Then brush again with your fan brush. If they look too much like stripes, brush lengthwise down the leaf to soften them, and then out from the center again.

Put the vein down the middle with med. green No. 2 + Raw Sienna, liner brush and thinner.

Before adding highlights, reinforce the dark colors where necessary and brush again with the fan brush, being careful not to brush over the center vein. Add the highlights with the softened pile of highlight green in the same manner as you did for the flowers. Use a very small amount of paint on the brush when you highlight the teeth along the edges (add a little thinner if necessary).

Finish the stems as before and then paint the three leaves on the right.

Where the center vein goes into shadow (upper left leaf of these three), make it darker by adding Raw Sienna to dk. green No. 2.

### THORNS

Paint the thorns with Burnt Sienna, liner brush and thinner. Where the thorns are in shadow, darken the lower part of them with some dk. green No. 1 or a little French Ultramarine Blue. Highlight the rest with Burnt Sienna + White, and then a lighter shade with a little yellow added. Blend the base of most of the thorns slightly into the stem colors.

### WATERDROPS

Follow directions in front of book. Be careful not to get the colors too dark.

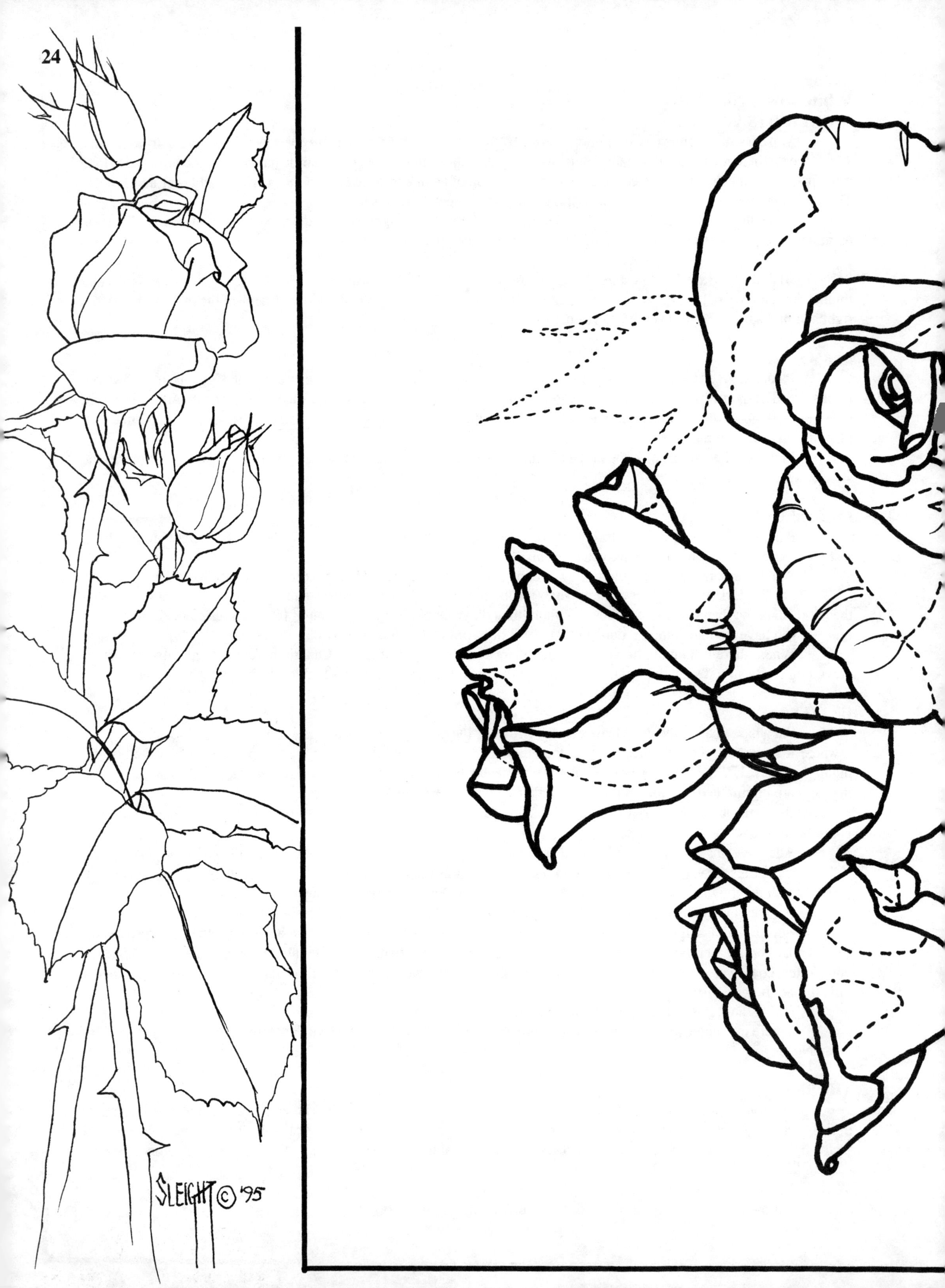
SLEIGHT © '95

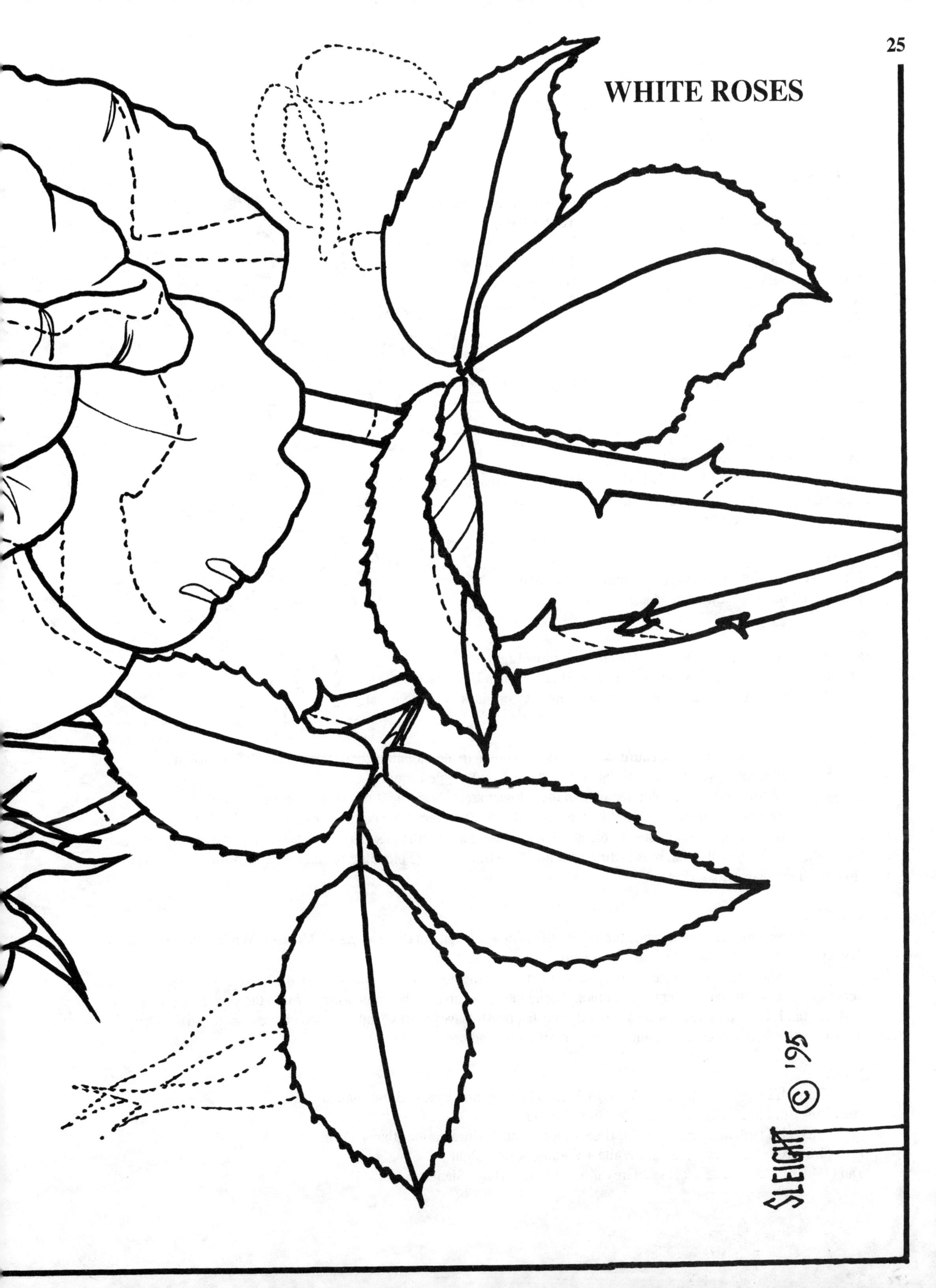
WHITE ROSES
SLEIGHT © '95

# Mt. Shuksan

**CANVAS:**  12 x 16 White

**PALETTE**

White
Cadmium Yellow Light
Cadmium Yellow Medium
Cadmium Orange
Cadmium Red Light
Raw Sienna
Cerulean Blue

French Ultramarine Blue
Yellow Citron (Weber)
Leaf Green Medium (Weber)
Terre Verte (Weber)
Burnt Sienna
Burnt Umber

**BRUSHES**

Flat or Filbert Bristle Brushes - No. 5 or No. 6 <u>and</u> No. 4 or No. 5
Small Bristle Fan Brush - No. 2 or No. 3
Mock Sable Cat's Tongue Brush - No. 4
Flat Mock Sable Brushes - No. 2 and No. 4 (or equivalent)
Mock Sable Liner - Preferable Long No. 4
Small and Medium Size "Bush" Brushes - Older brushes that have gotten bushy
Optional - No. 1 Flat Mock Sable Brush (approx. 1/8 inch wide)
   No. 2 or 3 Sable Fan Brush

**MEDIUMS**

Linseed Oil + Thinner or  Prepared Medium without drier
Liquin - (Winsor & Newton product)

**MIX:**

Cream (1/2 tsp)..................White + Cadmium Yellow Light
Lt. Blue (1 tsp)................. White + Cerulean Blue + French Ultramarine Blue
  Transfer the pattern to your canvas using grey or black graphite paper.

**SKY**

 Paint lt. blue mix in the entire sky from the top down to the mountain, except on the far left and right - stop a little above the mountain.  Use a No. 5 or 6 flat or filbert brush and a <u>little</u> Liquin.

 Work some cream mix into the blue in these lower areas, bringing it on down to the mountain.  Blend well.

 Add French Ultramarine Blue into the top of the sky (use very little paint to start with) and blend down.  If you're using a filbert brush, lay it on its side to blend.  If you're using a flat brush use an "X" - stroke with the end of the bristles. Brush the entire sky with a fan brush - first with an "X" -stroke if more blending is necessary, then finish with horizontal strokes all the way across.

**CLOUDS**

 These should be put in while the sky is still somewhat wet, but dried to the sticky stage. While you are waiting for the sky to dry a bit, you could mix the next colors.

 Use the small cat's tongue brush and cream mix (no medium) for the clouds.  Lay the brush slightly on its side and very lightly scrub the paint over the sky color.  Blend the lower area of the clouds slightly into the sky.  Brush very lightly with the fan brush - preferably a sable fan.  If your fan brush leaves marks (and you don't have a sable fan), try making a mini-fan our of your liner (see definition in front of book) and use it for this step.

**MIX:**

Dark Grey (1/2 tsp)........................White + French Ultramarine Blue + Burnt Sienna
Grey (1/4 tsp)..................................Dk. Grey + White
Med. Blue (1/4 tsp).........................Lt. Blue + more French Ultramarine Blue + Cerulean Blue
Pink (1/8 tsp)..................................White + Cadmium Red Light
Tan (1/4 tsp)...................................Grey mix + White + Burnt Sienna

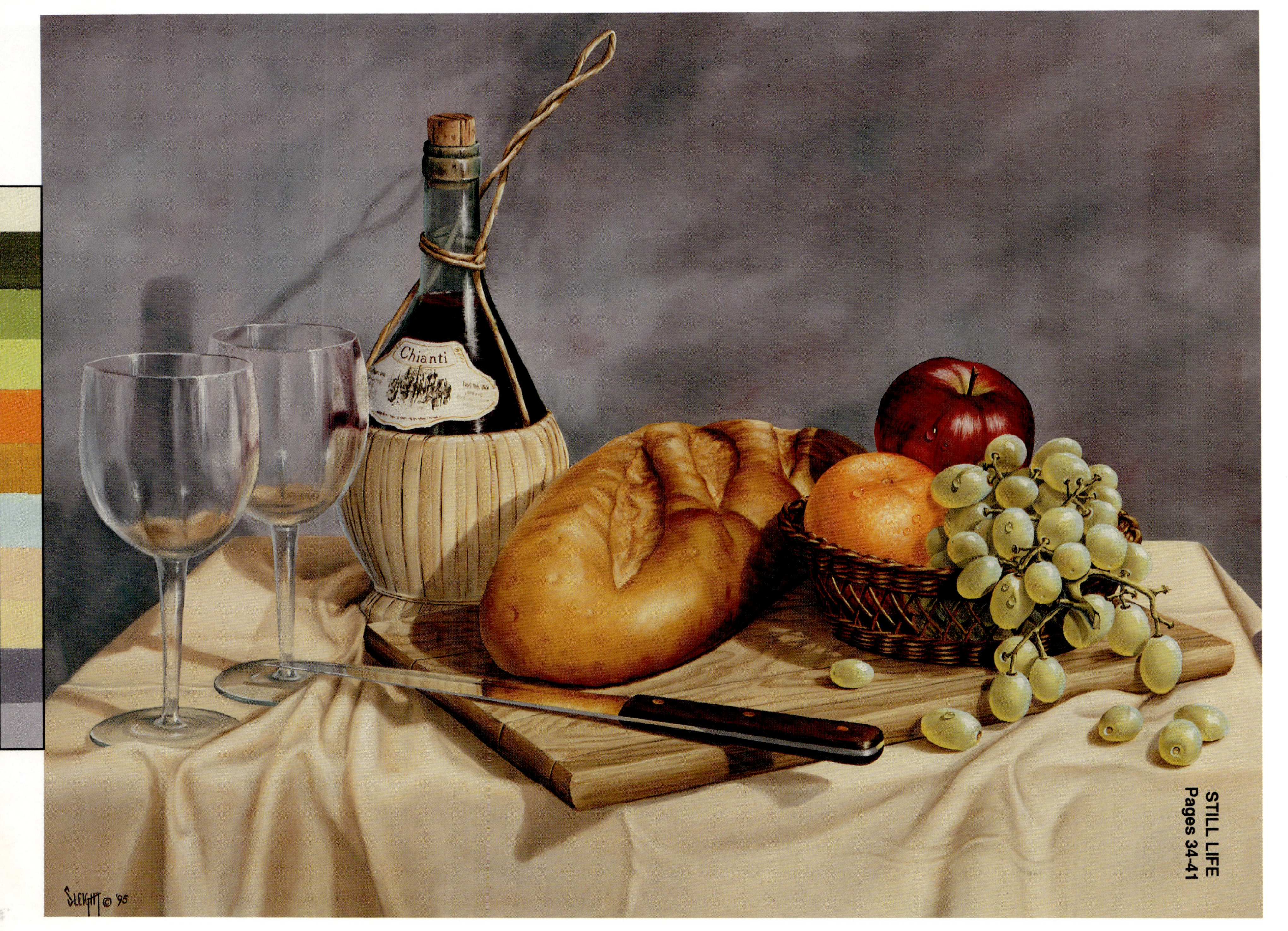

STILL LIFE
Pages 34-41
Chianti

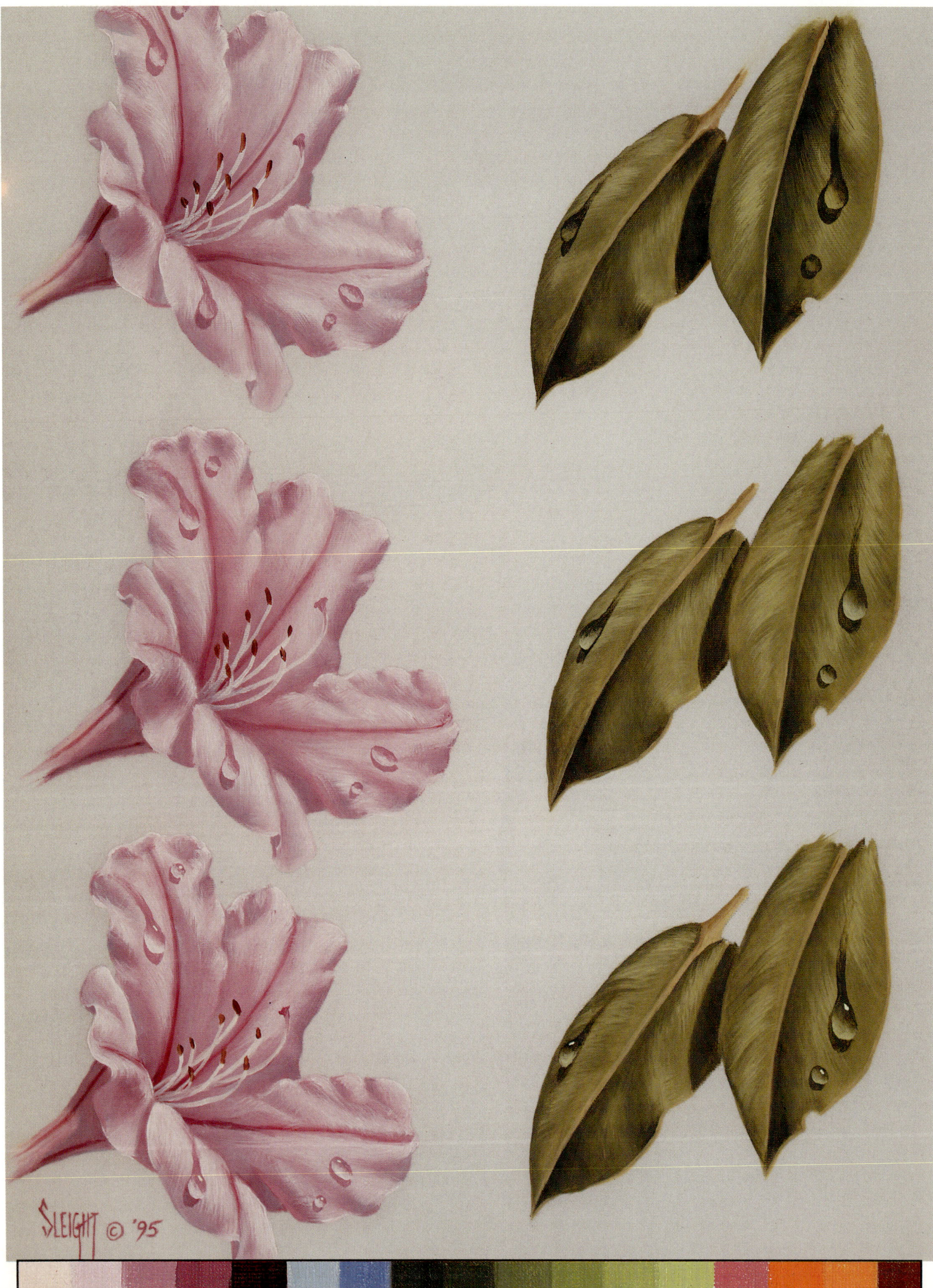

SLEIGHT © '95

## Mt. Shuksan continued
### MOUNTAIN

Using a small flat mock sable brush, Liquin and the grey mix, paint the mountain rock along the top of the mountain and down the first "block" of rock along the left side. Keep this smooth, but not too thin.

Paint the blue shadow snow next to the left side in the same way with the med. blue mix. Don't worry about the small bits or trails of snow on the rock yet, or the smaller rocks in the snow. These will be added later. Just concentrate on the larger blocks of rock and snow.

Fill in the sunny snow on the left side of the top and down the left side to the right of the shadow snow with the cream mix and Liquin. Use a smaller flat brush in the really small areas. Add some pink mix where the blue and "white" snow meet as a transition color.

Fill in the next group of rocks on the left side with the dark grey mix, leaving <u>small</u> cracks where the lines are within the rock. Do the same with the closer, darker rocks below the middle of the top. Then paint the snow (shadow and light) to the right and below these rocks. Continue this way across the mountain, but don't try to do too much at one time.

As soon as the first group of rocks (painted with the grey mix) starts to lose its shine, but preferably before it's completely dry, add the highlights. Use the chisel edge of a small flat mock sable brush and the tan mix (no Liquin or medium) to make short downward strokes over the grey. Be sure to leave some grey showing. If this picks up too much grey, let it dry some more and try again. Add a little White to a corner of the grey mix for "highlights" within the shadow areas of rock.

As each section of rock gets dry enough, add the highlights with the tan mix, closing the cracks as you do so. NOTE: Most cracks are where shadows are; <u>some</u> are where there is a trail of snow. Save these trails of snow to do later.

Blend the med. blue and pink mixes into the areas of sunny snow that have subtle, soft shadows. These are usually soft edged - a cat's tongue brush works well.

While you're waiting for the rock color to be dry enough for highlights, add the small rocks over the snow using your liner brush. Use the grey mix with a little dark grey added for the first section of snow on the left, the dark grey for all the rest. Also, add a <u>little</u> thinner so you can "draw" with your brush. Don't get the paint too thick or it'll be hard to add highlights later.

Once the highlights are done on the rock, you can add the trails and small patches of snow within the rock. Use your liner brush again, the snow colors (cream or med. blue) and thinner.

Add a little White and Cadmium Yellow Light to some of the tan mix for an extra highlight on selected areas of rock. Apply this with a liner brush and only to the very brightest area of rock - usually at the tops of "peaks".

Add a <u>touch</u> more French Ultramarine Blue and Cerulean Blue to some of the med. blue mix and put extra accents in some areas of shadow snow. Use a liner brush or other small brush. Don't overdo this and don't get it too dark.

### HILL ON LEFT

Fill in with the tan mix, leaving room at the bottom and on the lower left for the trees. Mix a <u>very</u> small amount of Cadmium Red Light into some of the tan mix. Brush this into some areas of the tan mix, then add some shading with the dark grey mix.

### MIX:

Dk. Green No. 1 (1/2 tsp)................................Terre Verte + French Ultramarine Blue
*Dk. Green No. 2 (1/4 tsp)...........................Leaf Green Medium + French Ultramarine Blue
Med. Green No. 1 (1/4 tsp)...........................Dk. Green No. 2 + White + Yellow Citron
Med. Green No. 2 (1/4 tsp)...........................Med. Green No. 1 + White + Yellow Citron
Highlight Green (1/8 tsp).............................Med. Green No. 2 + White + Yellow Citron
Grey-green (1/4 tsp)......................................Dk. Grey + Dk. Green No. 1

*Start with a larger amount of this mix (about 1 tsp) since you will need to make other mixes from it.

Add a touch of dk. green No. 1 to the dk. grey mix (not as dark as the grey-green mix) for the small trees on the hill on the left. This works best if you wait until the hillside is partially dry. Use the chisel edge of the smallest flat mock sable brush and make short downward (or upward) strokes-some clustered, some separate. Add some darker accents with the grey-green mix.

### DISTANT TREES

Paint the "ridge" of <u>distant</u> tress below the mountain with the grey-green mix. Use the larger flat mock sable brush and a <u>little</u> Liquin. Fill in the entire area with the same color first, painting the upper edge with irregular upward strokes. Then add a bit more dk. green No. 1 to the grey-green mix and add some darker, more detailed trees among the first group. Do this to some of the taller trees and add some shorter ones in front also. Turn the brush horizontally and use just the corner for the "branches" on these trees. Keep most of the trees on the left under the hillside darker for contrast.

If you can, let the painting dry overnight at this stage. It will be easier to put the darker trees in front.

Mt. Shuksan continued

**FOREGROUND TREES**

Use dk. green No. 1 and the No. 4 (3/8" wide) flat mock sable brush (no Liquin or medium). Lay the brush almost flat on your palette and load both sides of it, forming a good chisel edge. Hold the brush with the bristles vertical for the "trunk" and tap the paint on. Then turn the bristles horizontal for the "branches" (foliage) and tap, first with just the corner at the top of the tree, then with more of the brush in the bushier part of the tree (see illustration in front of book). Don't leave any thick paint on as that will make it harder to put highlights on later. If you must use Liquin, use very little since it weakens the covering power of the paint (makes it more transparent).

If the trunk of a tree is showing, paint it with a liner brush, Burnt Umber and thinner; then highlight the right side (when partially dry) with the tan mix. On the thicker, lower part of the trunk add a backlight along the left side with a darker mixture of med. blue (add French Ultramarine Blue + Cerulean Blue) - liner brush and thinner. Don't get this too light or it'll look like a highlight on the wrong side of the tree!

Paint the most distant dark trees, then the ground or bushes in front of them; then the next trees and the bushes and ground in front of them, and so on until you get to the water.

Where there are green bushes below the trees, extend the dk. green No. 1 further down. Then tap the bushes on with an older cat's tongue brush that has gotten bushy. Point the brush straight in at the canvas. Use med. green No. 1 very lightly, then med. green No. 2 on the right side.

**MIX:**

Dk Red (1/4 tsp).............................Cadmium Red Light + dk. green <u>No. 2</u>
Med. Red (1/8 tsp)..........................Cadmium Red Light + Raw Sienna
Lt. Red (1/8 tsp).............................Medium Red + Cadmium Orange
Yellow-orange (1/8 tsp)...................Cadmium Yellow Medium + Cadmium Orange

**BUSHES AND GROUND COVER**

Paint the dk. red mix into the red areas, adding Burnt Umber and dk green No. 1 for the dark side of the bush or shadows on the ground. Use the same bushy brush as before. When you need a crisper edge as on the top of the "hill", use the small fan brush and load both sides of it with paint like you did for the fir trees.

Highlight the red bushes and ground cover with the med. red mix, then the lt. red. Use the yellow-orange mix only for the closest and brightest areas. Tap these highlights on with the same bushy brush as before, using a <u>little</u> more paint.

For the more yellow bushes, use combinations of Cadmium Orange + Raw Sienna, Cadmium Yellow Medium + Cadmium Orange, and Cadmium Yellow Medium. Some bushes should be more orange than others. Also, tap a <u>little</u> med. green No. 1 or No. 2 into some of them.

The small sliver of ground color on the left is the tan mix + Burnt Umber.

Be sure to paint the bushes, trees and ground behind other trees and bushes before you paint the closer ones.

**TREES**

Let the fir trees dry a little before adding highlights. Then add them with your liner brush. Stroke it in the paint as you did the flat brush for the fir trees (no medium). This will create a very small flat brush. Tap it on the trees for highlights using the med. green No. 1, then med. green No. 2 (moving further to the right with each lighter color). Save the highlight green for the closest trees and bushes.

There should be a narrow strip of tan mix along the water line, with a shadow under it of Burnt Umber. Use your liner brush and thinner.

**SMALL ROCKS ON SHORELINE**

Use the lighter version of the tan made for the highlight on the mountain rock (tan + White + Cadmium Yellow Light), liner brush and thinner. Shade with Burnt Umber.

**DEAD TREE (on shoreline)**

Grey mix + White - liner brush and thinner.

**WATER**

Make a rough outline on the water of the reflected trees and red hillside with the grey mix and thinner (small brush). No detail - just vertical lines for the trees and a slightly diagonal line for the hillside.

Start painting with the mountain colors, roughly reflecting the <u>main</u> shapes and colors - no detail. Use a larger flat mock sable or a No. 4 or No. 5 stiffer bristle brush and a little Liquin. Add a little sky color (lt. blue mix + cream) in the left corner (behind foreground fir tree).

## Mt. Shuksan continued
### WATER continued

Next, add some grey-green just below the sketch for the darker green trees, overlapping the mountain colors.

Clean out any mountain colors that might be where the dark trees will go so the lighter paint won't weaken the dark green color (use flat mock sable brush and thinner).

Make a vertical stroke of dk. green directly under each tree above. Then turn the brush horizontal and make a zigzag back and forth across the vertical stroke all the way down to the tip, getting narrower towards the tip by not using all of the brush. For the smaller trees in-between the large ones, just make vertical strokes, filled in in-between. There should be no bare canvas showing between the reflection of the trees and mountain.

Next add the lighter trees and bushes in front of the bigger ones with the highlight green; then the yellow and orange bushes with Cadmium Yellow Medium and Cadmium Yellow Medium + Cadmium Orange.

Then fill in the red ground cover between the trees and bushes with the medium and dark red mixes. Add Burnt Umber for the darkest shadows and some green amongst the red with dk. green No. 2 and med. green No. 1.

Let this dry a bit, then add some highlight green into the right side of the more prominent large trees.

Reflect the trunks of the dead trees and the more prominent ones of the large trees using a vertical stroke with the chisel edge of your larger flat mock sable brush and Burnt Umber. Then add a highlight on the right side with the same brush and the lightened grey mix on the dead trees, highlight tan mix on the rest.

Remove any excess thick paint in the water area by lightly skimming it off with your knife. Blend the water with your fan brush or other blender brush (I prefer the fan because it gives me more control). First brush in the mountain and sky area (of the water) vertically. Clean and dry brush. Then brush vertically over the trees, then the red ground color, being careful not to drag the red down into the mountain or trees. Be sure to clean and dry your brush if you go back into the trees or mountain after brushing the red area. The water should be quite blurry. When you think you've done enough, get back from your painting and check it. Finish with very light horizontal strokes across the entire water. Reinforce any light trees and bushes that got blended entirely out and brush lightly again.

Let the painting dry awhile (but not completely) and then reflect the small rocks and the dead snag near the middle of the shore.

Brush these horizontally with a sable fan or a mini-fan made out of your liner brush.

When this is dry or almost dry, brush some med. blue mix horizontally across the water with your fan brush. This should not be thick paint - just skim the surface.

### FOREGROUND

The foreground is easiest to do if you let the water dry (at least overnight) first.

Paint the trees in the foreground first with dk. green No. 1 in the same way as the more distant ones, but with more attention to detail in the foliage. While this dries a little, paint the tan mix into the left foreground (add Liquin) and shade it with Burnt Umber.

Fill in below the trees on the right and over to the green brush in the middle with dk. green No. 1. Add some Burnt Sienna in the area of the red bush.

Use a liner brush, thinner and the dk. green No. 1 for the grass between the trees. Be sure this is fluid enough practice on your palette. The key to getting fine points on the grass is to pull the brush away from the canvas at the top of each stroke (thus releasing pressure).

Use an older bushy brush (larger than for the most distant bushes) for the tops of the bushes. This should be pointed straight at the canvas with the tail tipped slightly up. Tap very lightly, first with dk. green #1 (for green bush), then with med. green No. 1, med. green No. 2 and highlight green, working progressively upward.

For the red bushes, add dk. red mix over the Burnt Sienna, then med. red and lt. red. Use a liner brush, Burnt Umber and thinner for the branches. Add some extra foliage over the branches with your liner brush and the same red tones, then with Cadmium Orange and the yellow-orange mix.

Paint some lighter green grasses in front of the darker ones on the right.

The trunk on the tree on the left is Burnt Umber, highlighted with tan + Burnt Sienna, then tan.

Highlight the fir trees with your liner brush as before, but in more detail. If you pick up dark green when you add highlights, let it dry more first.

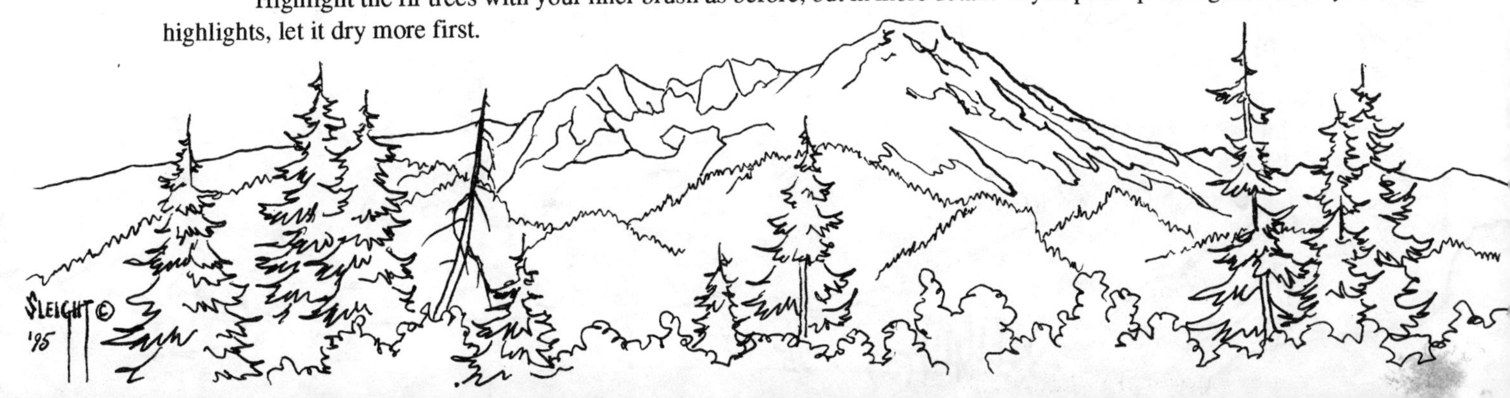

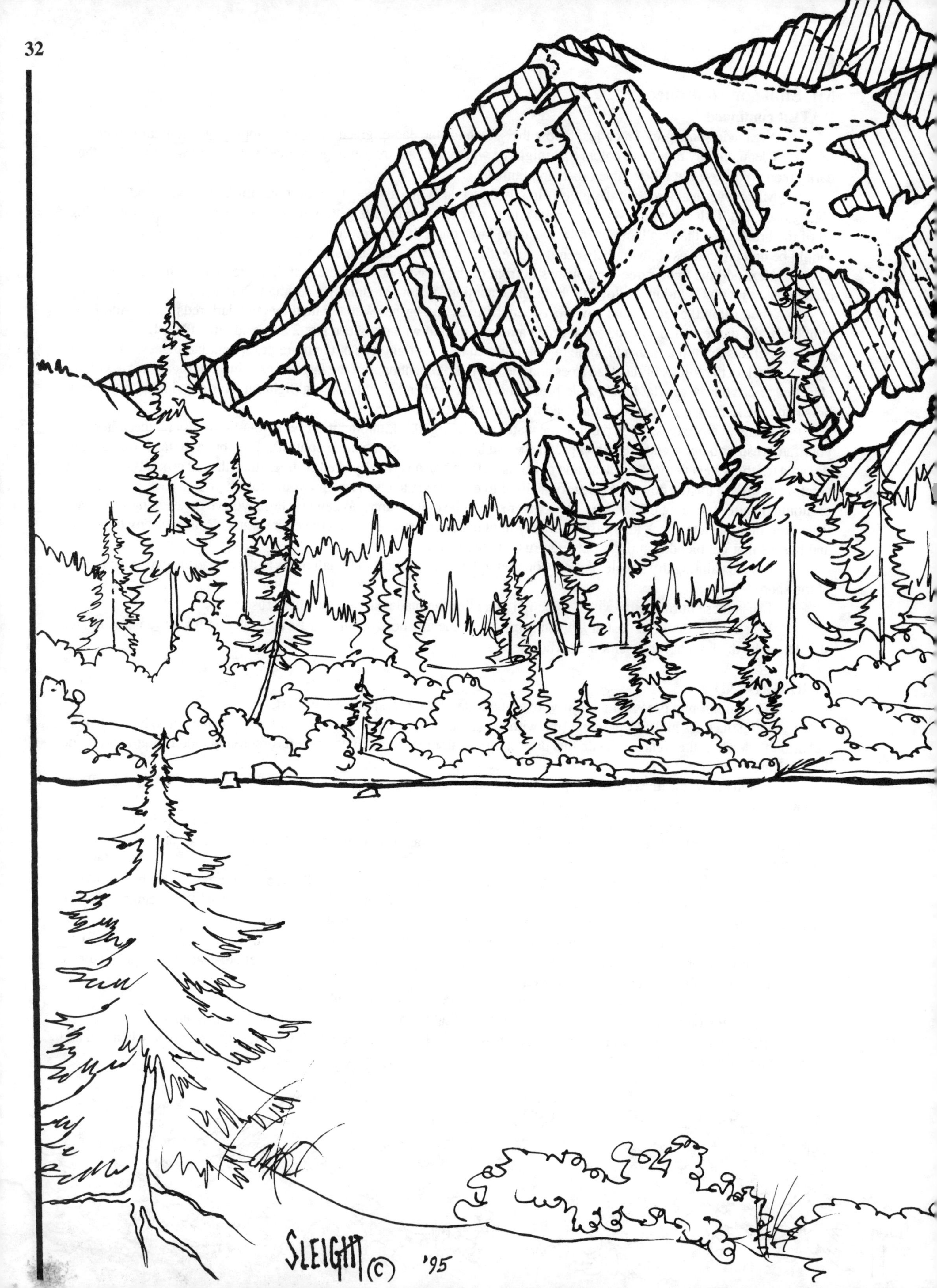
SLEIGHT © '95

# MT. SHUKSAN

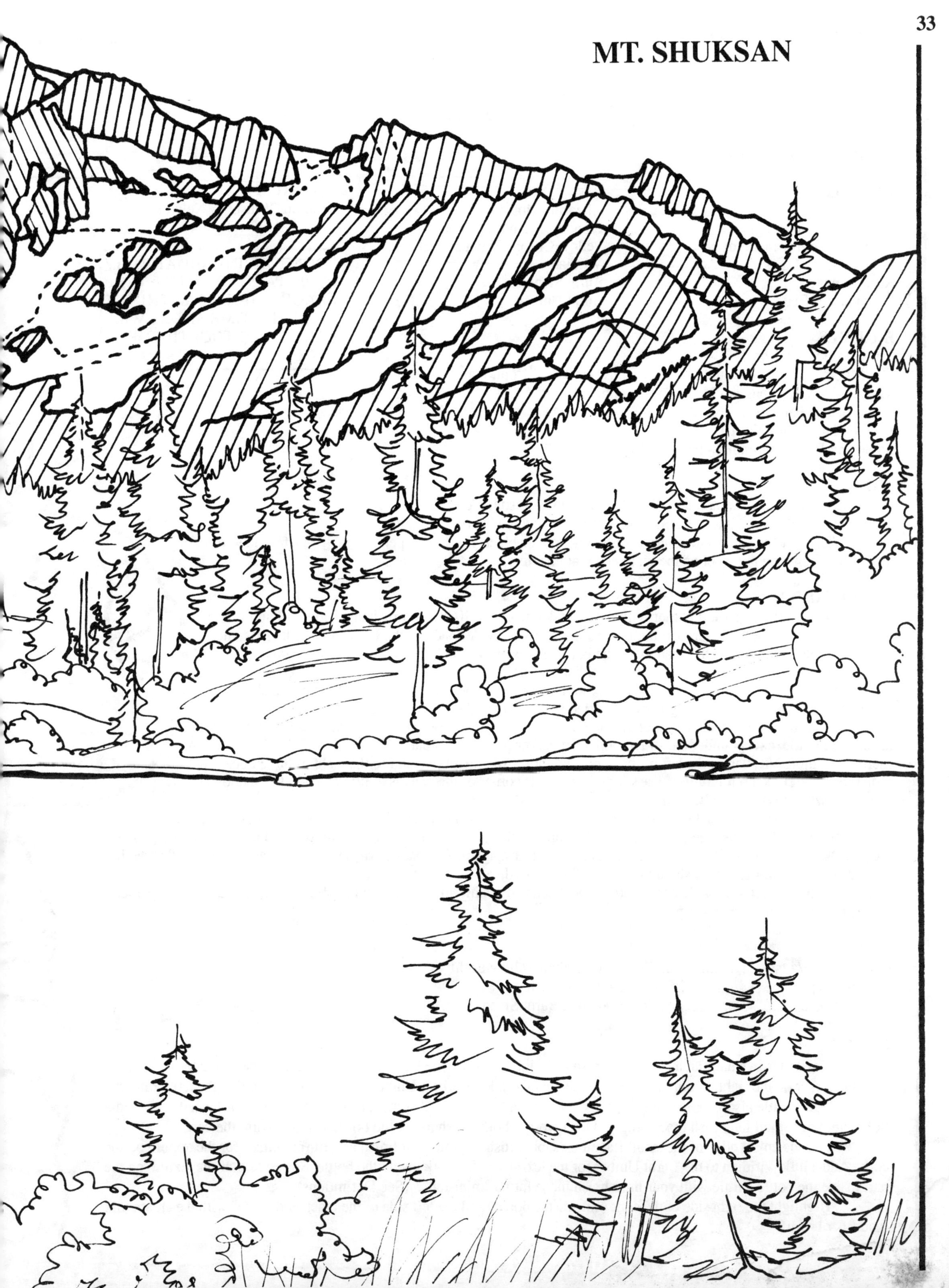

# *Still Life*

**CANVAS:** 16 x 20 White

**PALETTE**

White
Cadmium Yellow Light
Cadmium Yellow medium
Yellow Ochre
Raw Sienna
Grumbacher Red

Alizarin Crimson
French Ultramarine Blue
Yellow Citron (Shiva or Weber)
Viridian
Burnt Sienna
Burnt Umber

**MEDIUM**

Liquin (Winsor & Newton)
Linseed Oil + Thinner

> DON'T BE INTIMIDATED BY THIS PAINTING. JUST TAKE EACH SUBJECT WITHIN IT ONE AT A TIME AND IT WILL ALL COME TOGETHER FOR YOU.

**BRUSHES**

Liner- Preferably Long No. 4
Flat Mock Sables - No. 2 and No. 4 (or equivalent), No. 1 optional
Mock Sable Cat's Tongue - No. 4  (No. 6 optional)
Small Bristle Fan Brush - No. 2 or No. 3
Bristle Flat Brush - No. 10
Sable Fan Brush - Optional - No. 2 or No. 3

**MIX:**

Purple (2 tsp)................................ White + Alizarin Crimson + Viridian
Lavender (2 tsp)............................ Purple + White + touch Alizarin Crimson

Transfer the pattern to your canvas using grey or black graphite paper. <u>DON'T</u> transfer the writing or any of the design on the label on the wine bottle at this time.

**BACKGROUND**

Start in the upper left corner with the lavender mix, No. 10 bristle brush and Liquin.  Paint this down to the top of the table (around the glasses) and over to the left side of the bottle and a little past the top of the bottle.  Leave out the shadow of the bottle that is above the left glass.  As you go, add a touch more Alizarin Crimson in places and Viridian in others.  Be careful with both of these colors - a little goes a long way!  Add some purple mix in the lower left and for the shadow of the bottle above the left glass.  Wait until the background has dried a  little to put the shadow of the straw loop on.

Continue across the background, using more purple mix as you progress right.  Keep it lighter around the bottle, except under the straw loop, then darker nearer the bread.  Also, add more Viridian there.  Add more Viridian to the left of the apple and more Alizarin above and to the right of the grape. Don't over blend - keep it mottled.  Darken the upper left corner of the canvas a little and add the shadow of the straw loop with a smaller brush.

Soften the entire background with a fan brush or other blender brush.  Use a light "X" stroke first, then brush all strokes horizontally.  Brush lengthwise over the "loop" shadow first, then across very lightly.  If there is too much paint on the canvas, skim a little off with your palette knife, then brush again.  Get back a ways from your painting to decide whether it needs more blending.  There should be no hard lines or edges.

Using a flat mock sable brush and thinner, clean any paint off the foreground objects that has streaked over them. Refer to your pattern if necessary.

**MIX:**

Off- White (1/4 tsp)........................ White + Cadmium Yellow Light
Cream (1 tsp).................................. White + Yellow Ochre
Tan (1 tsp).....................................Cream + touch Burnt Sienna

**BOTTLE**

**Cork** - Use a small flat mock sable brush and Liquin.  Add some Burnt Umber to the tan mix for the top of the cork - a little darker on the right.  Paint the side with the tan mix, adding Burnt Umber as you move around to the left.  Paint the part inside the bottle also - same colors, but just a touch darker, then add some Viridian and a touch of lavender.  Blend a little with your small fan brush (use corner).  Don't worry about the shape of the bottle yet, just paint the cork.

Use the chisel edge of the small flat mock sable brush or your liner brush and Burnt Umber for the texture on the cork.  Add a little Viridian to the Burnt Umber for the texture on the cork inside the bottle.  Soften or blur the texture on the part inside the bottle a little with your liner brush made into a "mini-fan".  (See Definitions).

Highlight the right side of the cork (outside the bottle) and the left side of the crack and "hole" with the cream mix (and liner brush).

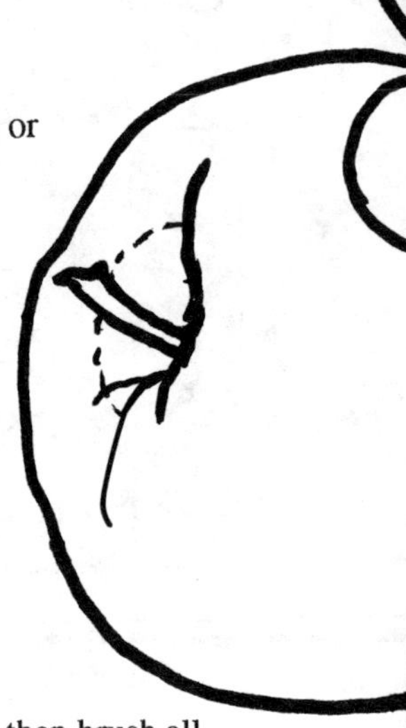

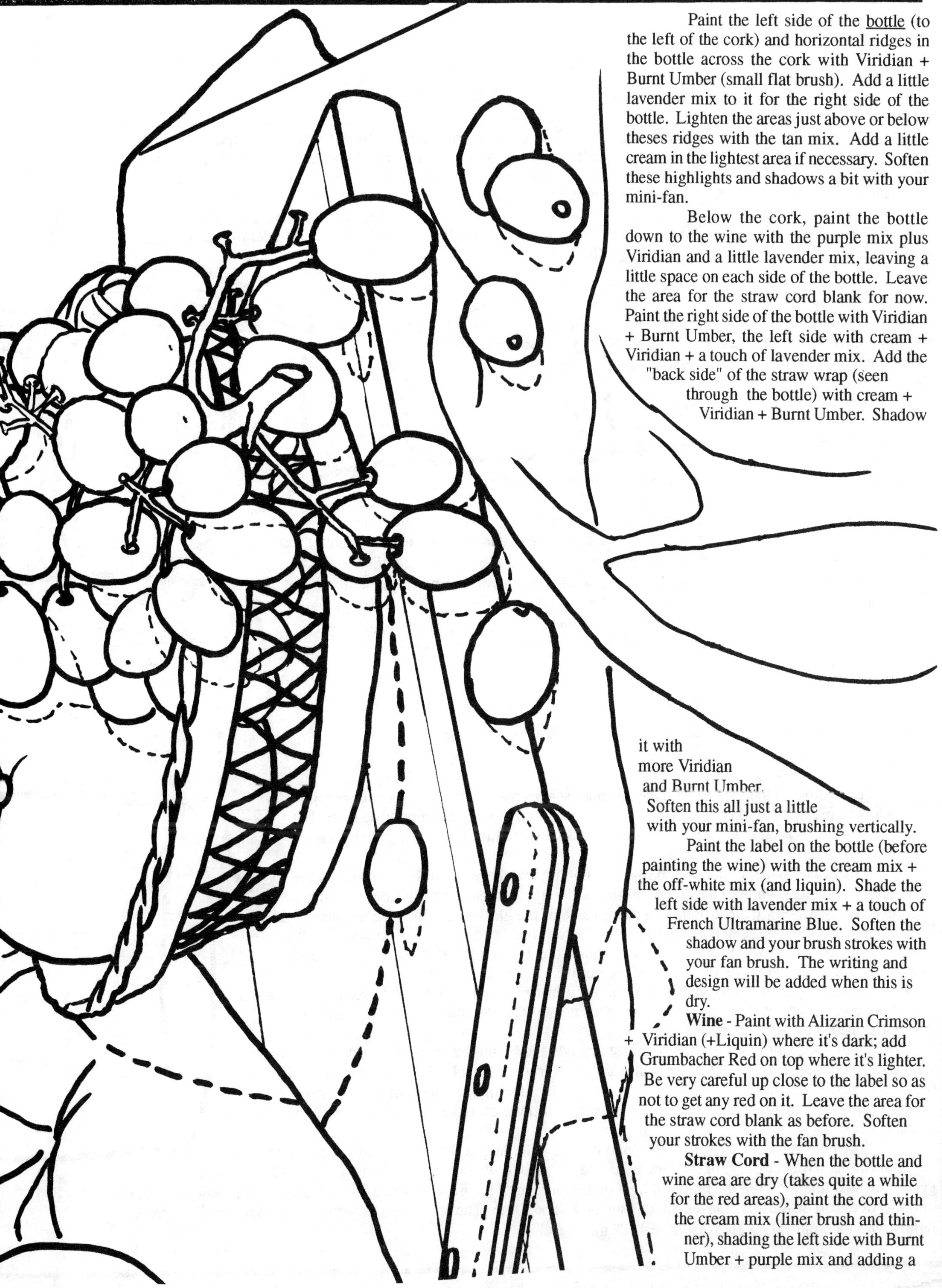

Paint the left side of the <u>bottle</u> (to the left of the cork) and horizontal ridges in the bottle across the cork with Viridian + Burnt Umber (small flat brush). Add a little lavender mix to it for the right side of the bottle. Lighten the areas just above or below theses ridges with the tan mix. Add a little cream in the lightest area if necessary. Soften these highlights and shadows a bit with your mini-fan.

Below the cork, paint the bottle down to the wine with the purple mix plus Viridian and a little lavender mix, leaving a little space on each side of the bottle. Leave the area for the straw cord blank for now. Paint the right side of the bottle with Viridian + Burnt Umber, the left side with cream + Viridian + a touch of lavender mix. Add the "back side" of the straw wrap (seen through the bottle) with cream + Viridian + Burnt Umber. Shadow it with more Viridian and Burnt Umber. Soften this all just a little with your mini-fan, brushing vertically.

Paint the label on the bottle (before painting the wine) with the cream mix + the off-white mix (and liquin). Shade the left side with lavender mix + a touch of French Ultramarine Blue. Soften the shadow and your brush strokes with your fan brush. The writing and design will be added when this is dry.

**Wine** - Paint with Alizarin Crimson + Viridian (+Liquin) where it's dark; add Grumbacher Red on top where it's lighter. Be very careful up close to the label so as not to get any red on it. Leave the area for the straw cord blank as before. Soften your strokes with the fan brush.

**Straw Cord** - When the bottle and wine area are dry (takes quite a while for the red areas), paint the cord with the cream mix (liner brush and thinner), shading the left side with Burnt Umber + purple mix and adding a touch of Raw Sienna in places.  Highlight with the off-white mix in the brightest places.

 **Basket** - Paint the basket on the bottle with the cream mix and Liquin, adding Burnt Umber and purple mix on the left side and in the cast shadow (to the left of the bread).  Keep the top edge of the basket lighter - add a little off - white - especially in the middle and right side.  (Be very careful up next to the red of the wine; if it keeps dragging into the basket, leave a crack until the red dries more, then fill it in).

Let this dry a little.  Then add Yellow Ochre and Raw Sienna for different tones, down the basket and a little lavender or purple mix (more Raw Sienna and purple towards the left side and in shadow).  Add crisper shadows between the "ratian" strips with a liner brush, Burnt Umber and thinner towards the left of the basket, Raw Sienna + Burnt Umber in the middle and right side.  Highlight just to the left of the shadow "line" with the cream mix on the left side of the bottle, off - white + cream mix on the right side, off - white on the top edge.  Add more Yellow Ochre + lavender to the cream mix for these highlights within the cast shadow area.  Use White + French Ultramarine Blue + Viridian for the backlight (see definitions in front of book) on the left side of the basket.

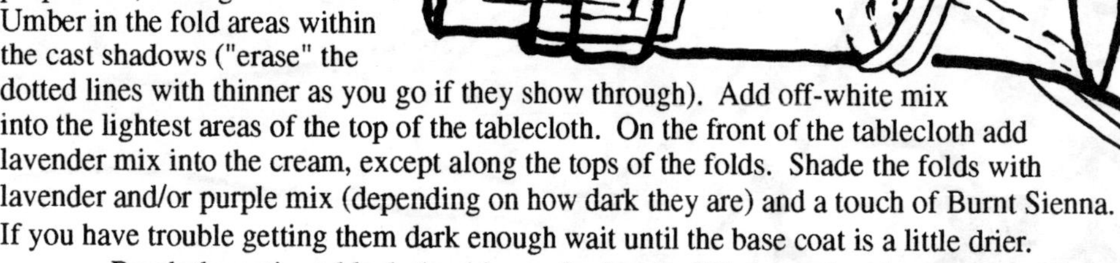


## TABLECLOTH

 Paint the tablecloth with the tan mix and Liquin, leaving a small crack where the fold lines are.  Then shade the cast shadow areas with more Burnt Sienna + purple mix, adding a little Burnt Umber in the fold areas within the cast shadows ("erase" the dotted lines with thinner as you go if they show through).  Add off-white mix into the lightest areas of the top of the tablecloth.  On the front of the tablecloth add lavender mix into the cream, except along the tops of the folds.  Shade the folds with lavender and/or purple mix (depending on how dark they are) and a touch of Burnt Sienna.  If you have trouble getting them dark enough wait until the base coat is a little drier.

 Brush the entire tablecloth with you fan brush.  When you brush across the folds, pretend you are brushing across the actual tablecloth and brush up and over the folds as though they are really three-dimensional.  Let this dry a little, then reinforce the darker shadows and folds if necessary and brush again.  Add a little cream mix along the tops of the folds and brush over it lightly with your mini-fan or sable fan.

## MIX:

Pale turquoise (1/4 tsp)................................. White + Viridian + lavender

## GLASSES

 Fill in most of the glasses with the lavender shades used in the background, keeping the shadow of the bottle darker as it is in the background and moving it over a little to the left of the background placement.  Leave very small cracks around the rim to be highlighted and shaded later.

 Reflect the shade of the label, basket (on bottle), and the wine in the right side of the right glass.  Add more white to the lavender mix for the lighter areas on the glasses (not the reflections of light).  For the backlights on the left side of the glasses, use the pale turquoise mix.  Reflect the tablecloth colors in the bottom of the glasses.  Just "chop" all these colors in with small and medium size flat mock sable brushes and Liquin (don't get paint too thin).  Use the purple mixture for the darker areas on the stem and base of the glasses.

 Let this dry quite a bit, but before it's too dry, brush it with a fan brush to soften and blur it a little.  Stay away from the wine color area first, then brush very carefully over it.  If it starts to streak, leave it alone for awhile and try again later.

 When the paint in the glasses is almost dry, add the highlights around the sides, bottom and stem (not rim yet) with the pale turquoise mix and liner brush.  Use a little thinner only if really necessary.  Brush this just slightly into the glasses with the liner made into mini-fan or a small cat's tongue brush.  Add a little more Viridian into the pale turquoise mixture for the rim around the base of the glasses.

 When the glasses are entirely dry, paint the rim with the purple mixture (add Viridian and Alizarin Crimson if necessary) in the dark areas and the pale turquoise in the light areas.  Use a liner with a good point and thinner.  Add the reflected light on the surface of the glasses with a "softened pile" (see definitions in front of book) of the off-white mix.  On the rim this should just be a line.  The other areas, however, should be brushed across very lightly with the mini-fan to give that "streaked" look.

# Rose Princess Iris

**CANVAS:** 14 x 18 White

**PALETTE**

| | |
|---|---|
| White | French Ultramarine Blue |
| Cadmium Yellow Medium | Yellow Citron (Weber) |
| Cadmium Orange | Leaf Green Medium (Weber) |
| Raw Sienna | Terre Verte (Weber) |
| Thio Violet | Burnt Sienna |
| Alizarin Crimson | Burnt Umber |

**BRUSHES**

Mock Sable Liner - preferably long No. 4
Flat Mock Sables - No. 2 and No. 4 (or equivalent)
Mock Sable Cat's Tongue - No. 4 (No. 5 optional)
Small Bristle Fan Brush - No. 2 or No. 3
Flat or Filbert Bristle Brush - No. 5 or No. 6
Flat Bristle Brush - No. 2 or No. 3
Optional - Sable Fan Brush - No. 2 or No. 3

**MEDIUM**

Liquin (Winsor & Newton)
Linseed Oil + Thinner

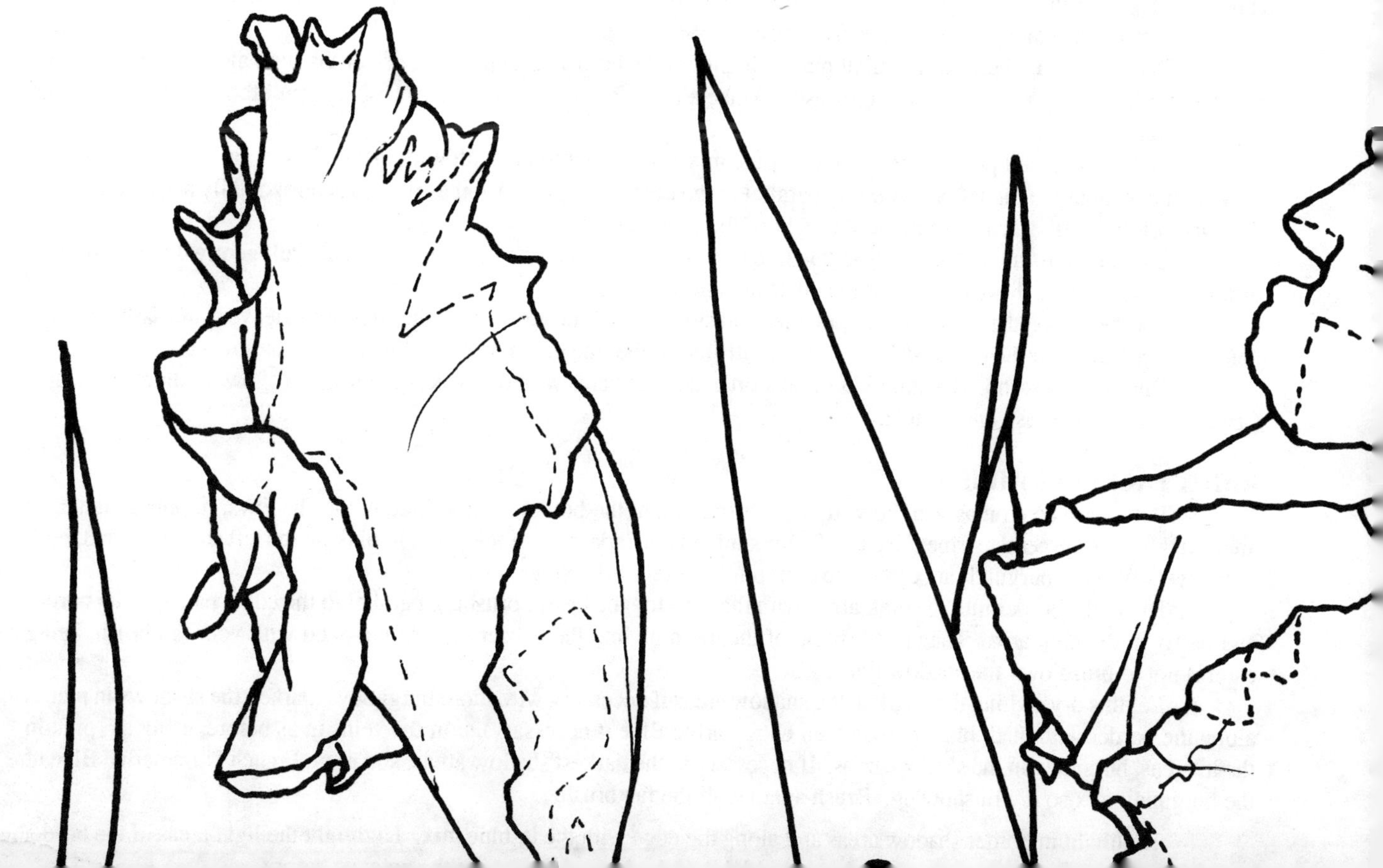

## Rose Princess Iris continued
### LEFT FALL - LEFT IRIS continued
Fill in the rest of the petal except for the darkest shadow areas with med. pink and Liquin, then dk. pink in the darker and shadow areas. Ignore the stripes on the shoulders (next to the beard) for now. Paint the lighter color "under" the stripes (lt. pink), adding some Cadmium Yellow Medium into it to warm it up. Add a little Cadmium Yellow Medium into the darker burgundy border next to this area. The orange tone just above the shoulder is Cadmium Yellow Medium + Alizarin Crimson - add a touch of Burnt Sienna where it needs to be darker.

Add some Alizarin Crimson with a touch of French Ultramarine Blue into the darkest shadows in the petal. Lighten some of the med. pink in the lightest areas with the lt. pink mix. Darken the shadows in the border where necessary with the med. blue mix. Be sure to keep the edges of the cast shadows crisp, but blend the edges of the others with your cat's tongue brush. Use this brush to blend some of the pink very lightly into the border color.

Brush the entire petal with your fan brush, brushing in the direction the petal is curving (being careful not to blur the edges of the cast shadows). While this is drying a little, work on more leaves or on the "tissue-like" wrap at the base of this iris.

### TISSUE-LIKE WRAP
Add more Raw Sienna into some of the White + Raw Sienna mixture used for the wrap on the bud. Then add lt. blue mix to "grey" the color. Paint the wrap with this color and Liquin (small flat mock sable brush) - darkening it with more Raw Sienna and med. blue mix toward the right side and below the wrinkles. Blend a little Burnt Umber into these areas also.

Just above the stem, mix some Yellow Citron and med. green No 1, then dk. green No. 1 for the stem with a little dk. green No. 2 on the left side. Soften a little with your fan brush.

After this dries a little, work some of the original, lighter White + Raw Sienna into the lighter spots. Work this in a bit so it won't be as bright as the highlights on the bud. Add a backlight on the right side of the stem with med. blue + French Ultramarine Blue (liner brush and thinner).

### LEFT FALL
When the paint has reached the "sticky" stage on the left fall, go back and reinforce the darks where necessary with the burgundy mix. Paint med. blue again into the shadowed areas on the border. Use the chisel edge of the smaller flat mock sable brush and the dk. pink to put the veins in (not a liner brush). Use the burgundy mix where the veins need to be darker.

Brush the petal again with your fan brush to soften these veins a little.

Use the softened pile of highlight pink to highlight the border (except where it's in shadow) along the edge and up into the border where needed (with liner brush). Make a mini-fan out of your liner brush and pull the highlight along the edge into the petal.

Make a softened pile of some of the lt. pink mix for the highlights within the petal. Use your liner brush to put a broken line in an arc to the left and roughly parallel to the center "stripe". Another line goes horizontally across the top of the curve of the petal, starting a little to the right of the center stripe.

Use the mini-fan to brush across this line in a curve matching the curve of the petal. Pull gently down first, then turn the canvas upside down and pull it the other direction.

For the line on the left of center, pull the right side to the right and sharply up. Be sure to leave some darker mauve color between this and the center stripe. Pull the left side of the line down to the left in a more shallow curve.

Once the right shoulder color has dried a little, add the veins with dk. pink + Cadmium Yellow Medium + Alizarin Crimson - use liner brush and thinner.

### RIGHT FALL - LEFT IRIS
Put a base coat on as you did with the left fall. Paint the border with lt. blue in the shadows, lt. pink in the light areas, lt. blue for the center stripe. Use the dk. pink mix in the dark areas of the petal, lt. pink on the left shoulder, med. pink in the rest. Add the burgundy mix over the dark pink where it is even darker.

Blend the border into the pink areas with the cat's tongue brush, brushing parallel to the edge, partly in the border and partly in the pink area. Then brush some of the dk. pink into the border. Brush the petal with your fan brush, being careful not to brush over the shadow lines.

Let this dry awhile, then darken the shadow areas if necessary with more burgundy. Darken the shadows in places along the border with med. blue (plus French Ultramarine Blue if necessary). Put the veins in as before, using dk. pink in the lt. areas, burgundy in the shadow areas. If necessary in the darkest shadow areas, add more French Ultramarine Blue to the burgundy mix so it will show up. Brush again with the fan brush.

Highlight in border shadow areas and along the edge with the lt. blue mix. Highlight the light areas of the border

## LEFT FALL - UPPER IRIS

Paint the blue border on the underside with lt. blue, on the topside with lt. pink.  Paint the underside of the petal with dk. pink, adding some med. pink in the left side and burgundy mix into the right side.  Add more burgundy (plus French Ultramarine Blue if necessary) into the darker shadows.

Paint the upper edge of the top side with dk. pink, then med. pink down to the border; lt. pink on the shoulder.  Add some lt. blue into the shadow area at the top of the shoulder, just under the upper petal.  Brush each section of the petal with the fan brush and let it dry awhile.

## LEFT STANDARD

Paint in the same way as the ones on the lower iris.  The small inside area just above the beard should be painted first with lt. pink.  Then add some Cadmium Yellow Medium into the lower part (not in the triangular area above it).  Paint Raw Sienna over the darker, more golden areas, then some med. pink mix.  Paint the triangular area just above this with lt. blue, then add a little med. pink in some places.  Brush all this well with the fan brush.  Keep it soft - no sharp edges.

## RIGHT STANDARD

Paint as previous ones.  Add some Cadmium Yellow Medium in the lower part.  Note that most of the light areas on the right side of this petal have a little shadow color (med. pink + lt. blue) in them.  The warmer pink shade you see in places is White + Alizarin Crimson.

## CENTER FALL

Paint as before.  Be sure to paint far enough up under the beard so all the canvas will be covered once the beard is painted.

## RIGHT FALL

Keep this petal much darker - use more of the burgundy mix.  On the shoulder, paint Cadmium Yellow Medium + Raw Sienna + touch of Alizarin Crimson.  When this is mostly dry, paint the veins over it with the burgundy mix.

## MIX:
1. Cadmium Orange + Alizarin Crimson (1/8 tsp)
2. No. 1 + burgundy mix (1/8 tsp)
3. Cadmium Orange + Cadmium Yellow Medium (1/8 tsp)
4. No. 3 + White + more Cadmium Yellow Medium (1/8 tsp)

## BEARDS

**Left Iris, Left Beard** - Start with color No. 2 (liner brush and a <u>little</u> thinner), beginning each stroke a little above the bottom of the beard.  Overlap this with color No. 1 as you work towards the left, then color No. 4.  These last strokes should slant down a bit more.  Come up under the darker strokes with lt. blue, under the lighter ones with pale blue.  Make some more strokes over these with a cream color (White + touch Cadmium Yellow Medium).  These strokes should be quite short and slanted to the left even more.  Extend the length of these strokes with color No. 4 but keep them shorter than the first ones. If they don't show up, wait for the previous strokes to dry a little and/or darken the previous strokes a little with some light blue mix.

**Left Iris, Right Beard** - Paint the same way but stay with just the darker orange colors and lt. blue mix.

**Right Iris** - Start with color No. 2.  Don't try to make too many individual "hairs".  They should be more mass color with a slightly uneven top.  Overlap these with color No. 1, starting a little lower and leaving a little of the darker color showing above.  Repeat this with color No. 3, leaving some space in the middle for the light area.  Start bringing these (the No. 3) strokes down the sides a little; change to color No. 4 and come further down the sides.

In the light area in the middle, start with pale blue (these are the lower parts of the orange "hairs", not separate "hairs" and a few strokes of lt. blue; then the cream mix below.  Add some color No. 4 at the tips of the cream strokes if they don't match up with the previous strokes.  Add a few very short orange (No. 4) strokes in the middle (these are some hairs coming straight out).

## WATERDROPS

Follow direction in front of book.  Be careful not to get the colors too dark.

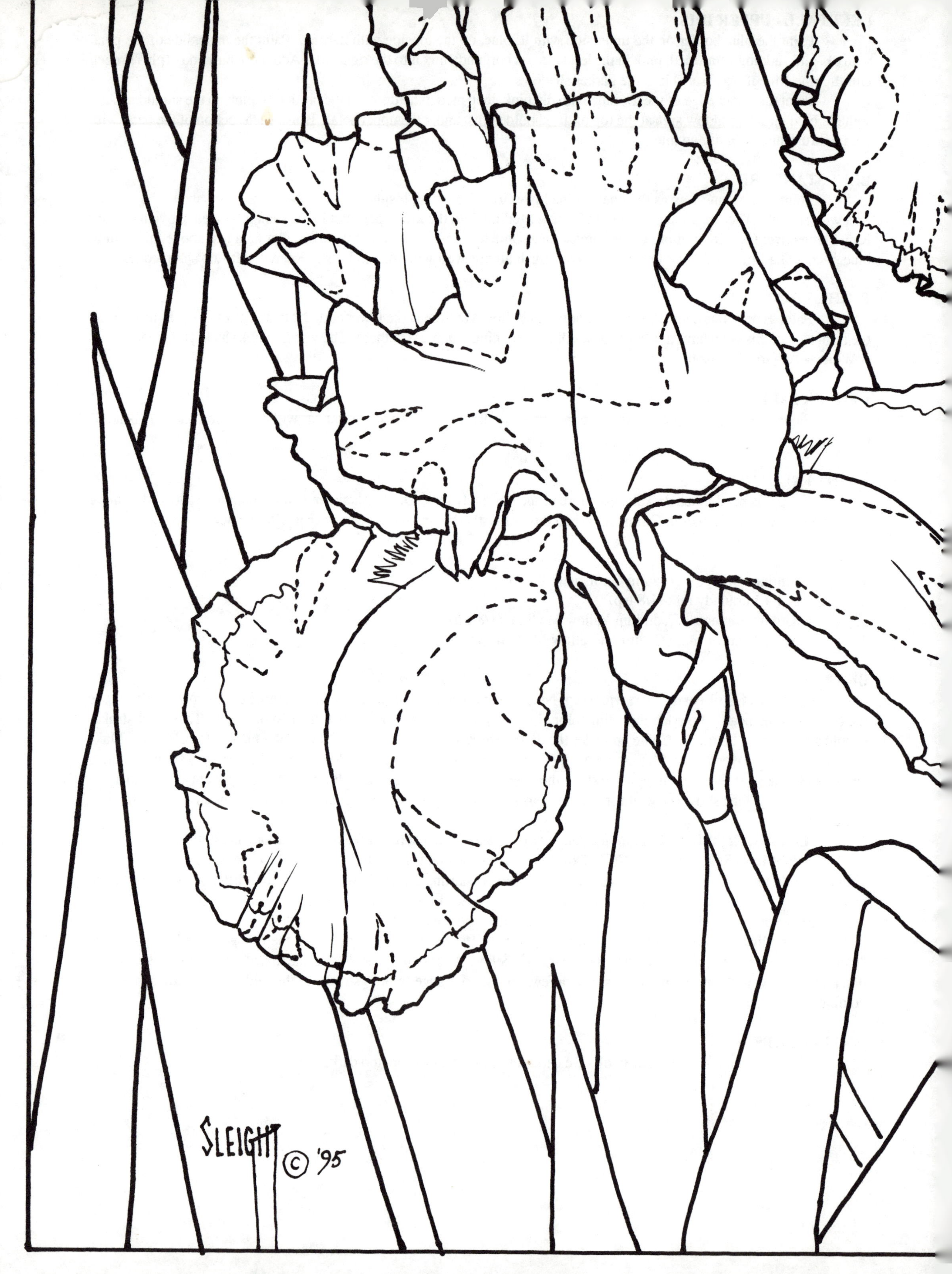

SLEIGHT © '95

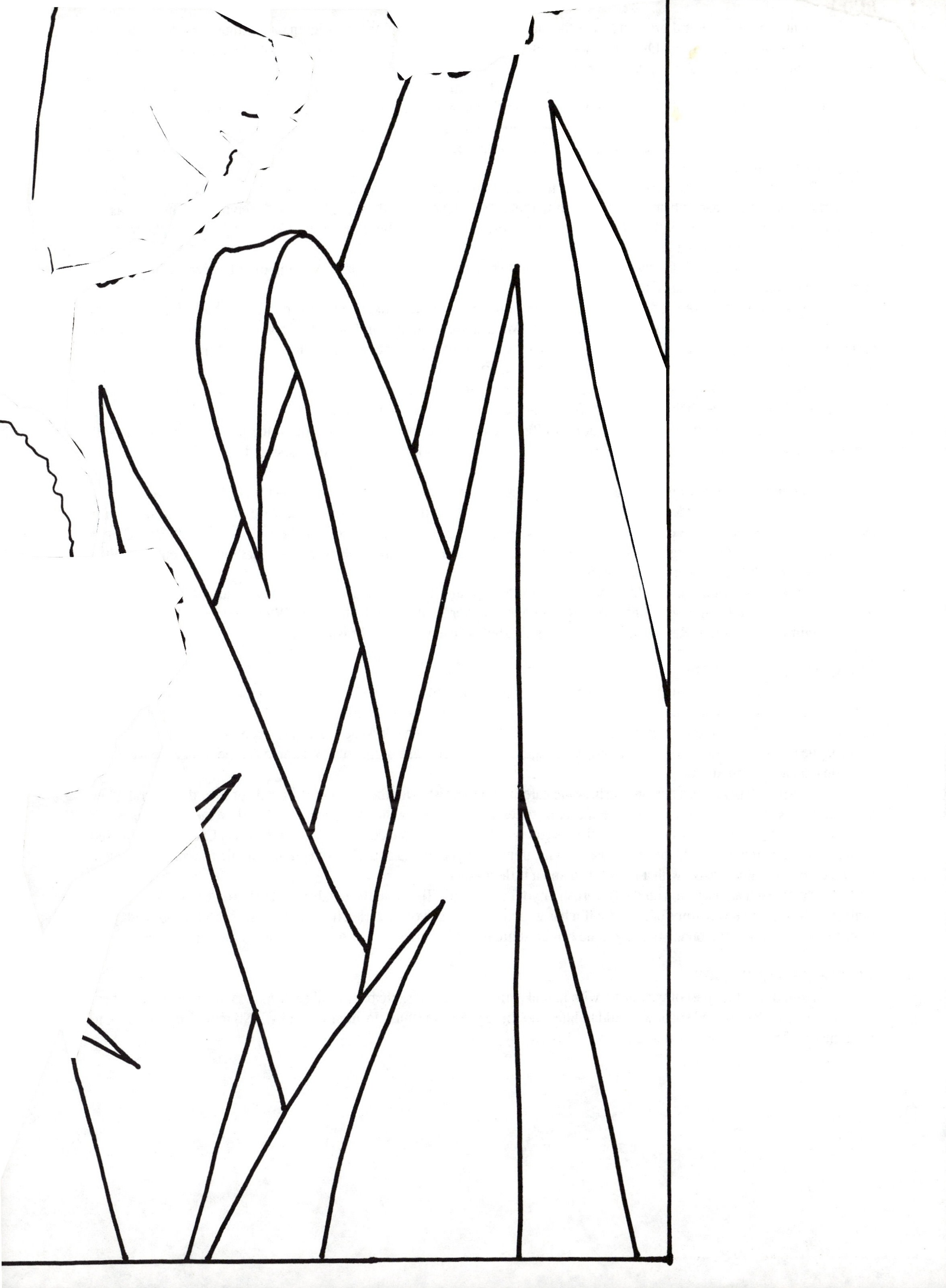

Paint the large central area and the other lightest areas with lt. pink and Liquin. Continue this down into the yellow/green area at the bottom. Overlap it with some med. green No. 2 mixed with a touch of med. pink and some more Yellow Citron. Add a little Raw Sienna over it.

On the lower right side (where it is darker), use med. green No. 1, Yellow Citron and a touch of dk. pink. Where the darker shadow is (at the top of this lower right section), add some Alizarin Crimson and French Ultramarine Blue. Use dk. green No. 2, then dk. green No. 1 for the darker green veins. For the lighter shadow near the left of the bud (to the right of the big "ruffle") use med. pink and lt. blue, adding a little of the yellow/green color into the lower area of the shadow as well as a touch of dk. pink.

Paint the med. pink areas of the bud with the med. pink mix and the darker ones with dk. pink mix. Leave only the very darkest burgundy shades blank. Before adding this color, blend some lt. or med. blue into the more mauve areas. A cat's tongue brush works well for this. Then paint the darkest areas with the burgundy mix. On the right side of the bud, use more French Ultramarine Blue in the mix.

Brush each area with the fan brush to blend and smooth out the brush strokes, using only the corner in the small areas. Where that won't fit, use your mini-fan.

Highlight with a softened mixture (see definition) of highlight pink. Paint one relatively thick line diagonally across the main part of the bud (down and to the right). Make a mini-fan of your liner brush and brush across the line down to the left (very softly) in a slight curve. Then brush up to the right across the line (turn the painting if necessary). Nearer the bottom right of the line, the stroke should be curved more sharply.

Another highlight goes along the edge of the big "ruffle" on the left. In some places this remains a line; in other places it should be brushed (with the mini-fan) into the petal. Don't get this highlight too thick.

Add a backlight on the underside of the ruffled petal and on the lower right side of the larger "main" petal with White + Alizarin Crimson (not too light). You don't need to make a softened pile of this, just add some thinner with your liner brush.

Highlight the yellow/green area with the highlight green + Yellow Citron + White + touch Raw Sienna.

Mix a very light shade of White + Raw Sienna. Paint the "tissue-like" wrap at the base of the bud with this mix leaving slight cracks where the lines are. Add a little dk. green No. 2 below the left edge of the bud. Shade with Raw Sienna along the lines and along the right (shadow) side. Blend some med. blue into the Raw Sienna shading. Soften this a little with your fan brush (use corner in small areas).

Let this dry awhile, then add a touch of Burnt Sienna and Burnt Umber in the darkest shadows with your liner brush. Make a mini-fan out of your liner brush to soften this darker shade. Add a little more White and a touch of Cadmium Yellow Light to the White + Raw Sienna mixture for highlights (use your liner brush and thinner).

## STANDARDS - LEFT IRIS

Paint lt. pink mix in all the lightest areas, use a flat mock sable brush and Liquin. Fill in the shadow areas with the lt. blue mix - add some pale blue in the lighter blue areas, lt. or med. pink in the mauve areas. Blend in a touch of White + Cadmium Yellow Light in the upper left petal where it looks warmer. The darkest shades are deep pink + med. blue. The cat's tongue brush works well for this shading. Use Liquin on the first "base" coat only. When you're blending into wet paint you don't need more medium.

Brush each petal with the fan brush, being careful not to brush over the edges of the petals or over the crisp shadow lines. Let this dry awhile, then reinforce the dark tones as necessary with more deep pink and/or med. blue mix. If necessary use a little burgundy mix in the darkest shadows. Mix a lighter shade of the White + Alizarin Crimson you mixed for a backlight on the bud. Add this in the areas on the upper right petal and at the bottom on the middle (larger) petal where it is much pinker. Put this on with a liner brush and a little thinner.

Brush each area again with the fan brush or your mini-fan. Highlight the petals with the softened pile of highlight pink mix. Add a few more drops of medium if it has gotten thick since you last used it. Blend these highlights out with your mini-fan as you did in the bud. (Highlight the brightest areas - sometimes along an edge, some on the top of a curve).

## LEFT FALL - LEFT IRIS

Paint the lighter part of the border with lt. pink, small flat mock sable brush and Liquin. Leave small cracks where the lines are that determined shadows. Add lt. blue into these shadows (thus closing the cracks). No more Liquin. Paint lt. pink into the "stripe" down the middle under the beard.

## Rose Princess Iris continued
### BACKGROUND continued

Test the upper part of the canvas with your fan brush to see how dry it is. Brush lightly with an "X"-stroke; if the paint streaks and feels slippery, you can wait a little longer to blur it out. If it feels sticky or a little "stiff", continue to brush with an "X" -stroke until you get to the fresher paint that is more wet. If necessary, brush the (background) leaves lengthwise first, then very lightly across. As the rest of the canvas gets to the "sticky" stage, blur it out too. Finish with horizontal strokes across the canvas.

**Background Flowers:** Paint the upper part of the bud on the left (behind the leaves) with the med. pink and Liquin and shade it with the burgundy mix. The lower part between the two leaves is Raw Sienna + White (not too light), shaded with a touch of Burnt Sienna and Burnt Umber. Don't get too busy with this bud as not very much shows.

Paint the upper part (the standards) of the flower in the right background with the lt. pink mix and Liquin. Shade it with the dk. pink mix and med. blue (no more Liquin). Let this dry awhile, then shade the darkest areas with the burgundy mix.

While you are waiting for that to dry some, paint the lower petals (the falls) on the right with the burgundy mix. Leave a little room for the edges. Paint them with the med. blue mix and blend slightly into the burgundy above (be careful - the burgundy can take over).

Paint the part of the falls in the diamond shape between foreground leaves with medium pink, shading it with the deep pink (+ more Thio Violet if necessary). Use lt. blue for the stripe down the middle. Brush within each petal carefully with your fan brush - use the corner in small areas - to smooth out the paint and blur a little.

As soon as the lower part of the background gets to that "sticky" stage, brush around the edges of the flowers to blend into the background a bit; then brush with the X-stroke as before, finishing with horizontal strokes across everything.

Use the larger flat mock sable brush (or the one with the best chisel edge) and thinner to clean off the paint that has streaked over the foreground flowers and leaves. Refer to your pattern if you can't see your lines.

### LEAVES

Start with the tallest leaf to the left of the bud. Paint the top part with med. green No. 2, the larger flat mock sable brush and Liquin. Keep the paint smooth - no thick paint - but not too thin. Fill in the lower part of this leaf with med. green No. 1 + dk. green No. 2, keeping it darker on the right side. Add dk. green No. 1 + dk. green No. 2, keeping it darker on the right side. Add dk. green No. 1 along the right side and in the shadowed area under the top part. Don't worry about the ridges yet - they will be added later. Brush the leaf vertically with your fan brush (held with bristles vertical), being careful not to brush over the edges.

Fill in the two leaves below and to the left of this one with the med. green mixes, adding a little dk. green No. 2 along the right sides and near the bottom, and some lt. green on the left side of the top leaf. Ignore the cast shadows for now, we'll add them when the leaves are dry. Brush these leaves with the fan brush as before.

Remember to use Liquin when painting in a base coat. It is usually not necessary to use it in later steps unless the base coat has gotten too sticky.

When the base coat has dried to the sticky stage on the leaves, reinforce the darks (or lights) where necessary. Then use the larger flat mock sable brush with the bristles held vertically to put the ridges on the leaves. Use a color one shade darker than the color of the leaf it's on. Be sure you don't space the ridges too evenly. Also make some thicker than others by pressing harder with the brush. Finish the ridges on the tall leaf and brush lightly with the fan brush before working on the other two leaves.

Make a softened pile (see definitions in front of book) of some of the highlight green. Use your liner brush to put the highlights on the leaves, primarily on the edges. The tall leaf has a highlight across it just before the bend. Put a line of highlight color across the leaf, then brush across the line with your mini-fan (see definitions), first in one direction, then in the opposite direction (turn painting if necessary). Some highlights along the edges of leaves remain a line, others get brushed lightly into the leaf.

The rest of the leaves are painted in the same manner, except use more lt. green for the lighter leaves and add more White and Yellow Citron to the lt. green for the very brightest leaves in the center of the painting. A few leaves have a touch of Raw Sienna added to the tip. In general, it's a good idea to finish a leaf that is behind a flower before painting the flower.

When the leaves are dry, paint dk. green No. 1 or No. 2 over the cast shadow areas depending on how dark the leaf underneath is. If the shadow is painted with dk. green No. 2, add a little dk. green No. 1 where the ridges continue through it. If this doesn't show up enough, add some med. green No. 1 or 2 and French Ultramarine Blue to it. If the shadow is dk. green No. 2, paint some dk. green No. 1 where the dark lines between the ridges are (within the shadow).

Brush lightly with the mini-fan in the shadow area only.

**NOTE:** Before painting any of the light areas in the foreground flowers, use a little thinner to lighten the lines inside each petal so they won't show through.

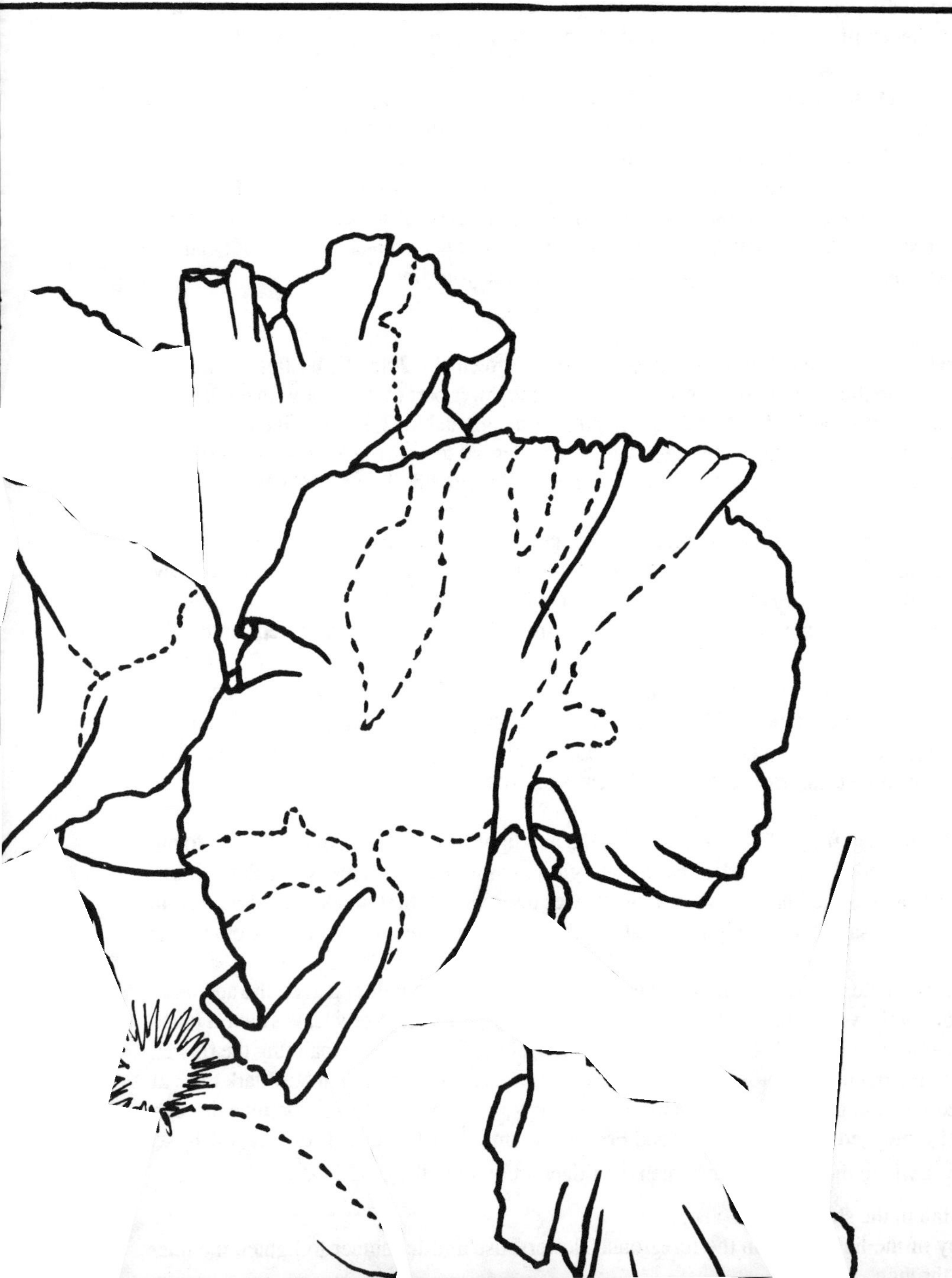

Transfer the pattern to your canvas using grey or black graphite paper.

Using a liner brush or small flat mock sable, sketch in the background flowers with Raw Sienna and thinner (no thick paint).

**NOTE:** The upper petals on an iris are called the <u>STANDARDS,</u> and lower petals are the <u>FALLS</u>.

**BACKGROUND**

Start in the upper left corner with the pale blue mix, No. 5 or No. 6 flat or filbert bristle brush and Liquin. Paint this across the top of the canvas and down about 4 inches in the middle - a little further on the sides. Add a little dk. green No. 1 to the light blue mix and overlap the pale blue. Using the same brush, make some strokes simulating leaves, some just random shapes. As you work down the canvas, start, using more dk. green No. 1 without the blue added and also some of the other mixed greens except the highlight green. When you get down to the background flowers, work around them and finish the rest of the background between the leaves and flowers. Add a little Raw Sienna in places where you see a little gold tones.

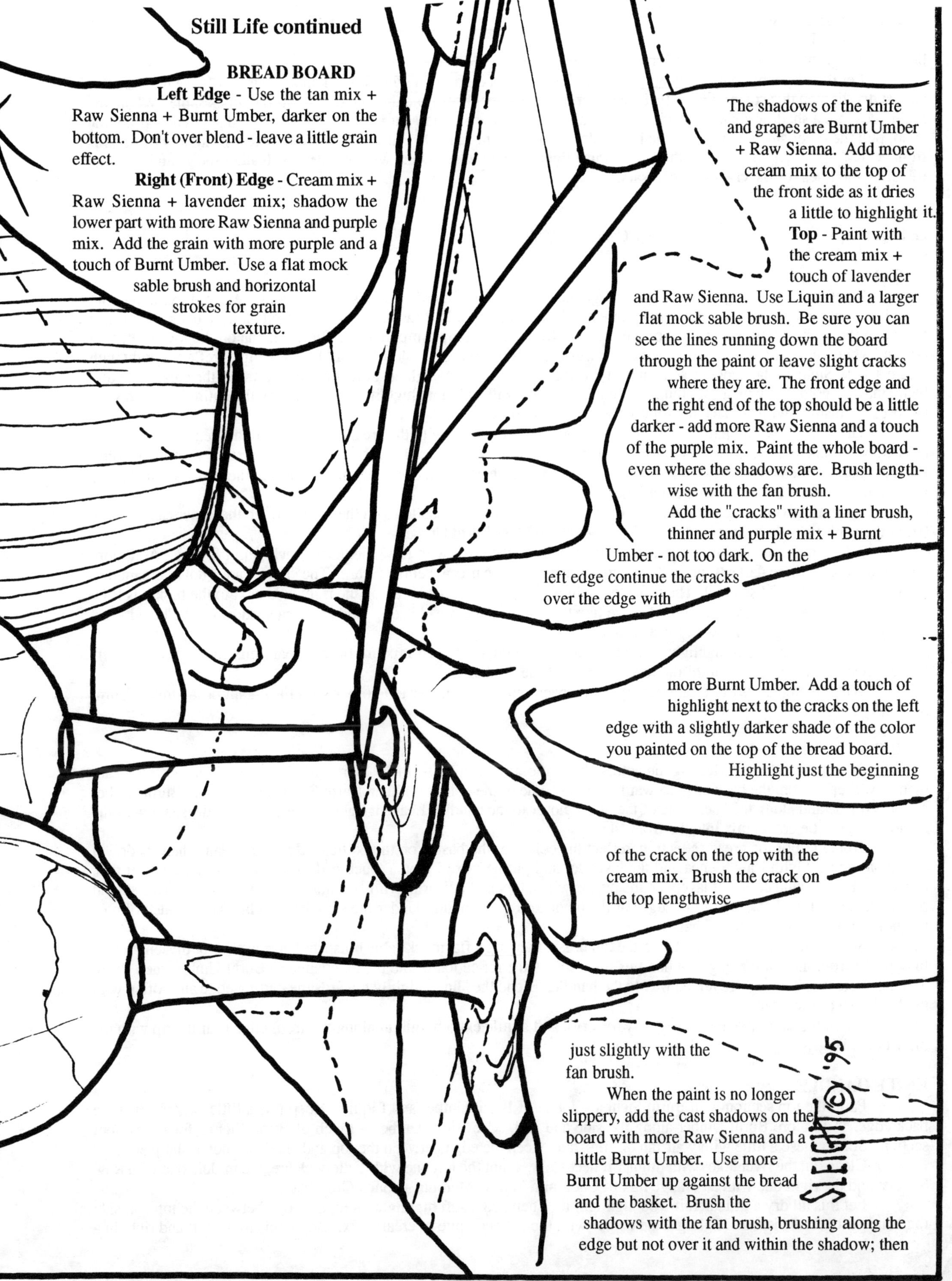

## Still Life continued

### BREAD BOARD

**Left Edge** - Use the tan mix + Raw Sienna + Burnt Umber, darker on the bottom. Don't over blend - leave a little grain effect.

**Right (Front) Edge** - Cream mix + Raw Sienna + lavender mix; shadow the lower part with more Raw Sienna and purple mix. Add the grain with more purple and a touch of Burnt Umber. Use a flat mock sable brush and horizontal strokes for grain texture.

The shadows of the knife and grapes are Burnt Umber + Raw Sienna. Add more cream mix to the top of the front side as it dries a little to highlight it.

**Top** - Paint with the cream mix + touch of lavender and Raw Sienna. Use Liquin and a larger flat mock sable brush. Be sure you can see the lines running down the board through the paint or leave slight cracks where they are. The front edge and the right end of the top should be a little darker - add more Raw Sienna and a touch of the purple mix. Paint the whole board - even where the shadows are. Brush lengthwise with the fan brush.

Add the "cracks" with a liner brush, thinner and purple mix + Burnt Umber - not too dark. On the left edge continue the cracks over the edge with more Burnt Umber. Add a touch of highlight next to the cracks on the left edge with a slightly darker shade of the color you painted on the top of the bread board. Highlight just the beginning of the crack on the top with the cream mix. Brush the crack on the top lengthwise just slightly with the fan brush.

When the paint is no longer slippery, add the cast shadows on the board with more Raw Sienna and a little Burnt Umber. Use more Burnt Umber up against the bread and the basket. Brush the shadows with the fan brush, brushing along the edge but not over it and within the shadow; then

## Still Life continued
### BREADBOARD continued

brush very lightly across the light and shadow areas.

Let this dry a bit, but not completely; then put the wood grain on with Raw Sienna + purple. If the undercoat is almost dry, lighten this color with a little lavender mix. Use a liner brush and thinner, or a small flat mock sable. Where the grain goes into a shadow area, add some Burnt Umber to the Raw Sienna + purple mix. Leave one edge of each grain line crisp; pull the other side slightly into the base color with the mini-fan. Do each section of the board separately (section is from "crack" to "crack"). Brush with the fan brush lightly lengthwise. Don't wipe it out - just feather the grain in a little. Redefine the lines for the cracks if necessary.

### MIX:
Gold (1/4 tsp) ................. Yellow Ochre + Cadmium Yellow Medium

### BREAD

Paint the entire bread loaf except the lightest areas and the "cuts" (where surface is more textured) with the gold mix. Use a medium to large size flat mock sable brush and Liquin. Add Raw Sienna into the next darkest areas, then Burnt Sienna in the darkest (still staying out of the "cuts"). Blend some purple mix into the Burnt Sienna on the lower left side (around where the bottle basket and breadboard meet). Just above this on the left side, add a backlight of reflected light with cream + Raw Sienna + lavender mix. Don't get this too light. Fill in the lightest areas on the bread with the cream mix and blend into the gold mix with a cat's tongue or fan brush. We will add more highlights later. Brush the entire loaf with your fan brush, finishing with strokes that follow the rounded contours.

The "cut" areas are painted with short dabbing strokes - first with the cream mix in the light areas, then the gold mix, Raw Sienna and Burnt Sienna until all but the darkest area is covered. Don't buildup any texture with thick paint. Paint the darkest area on the right of the "cuts" with Burnt Sienna + touch of Burnt Umber. Soften these areas just slightly with your fan brush, but don't wipe out all the texture effect.

Paint more Burnt Sienna and some Burnt Umber into the cast shadows on the bread. Keep the upper cast shadow (from the apple) a little lighter (add some Raw Sienna, use less Burnt Umber).

Add some more texture into the smoother areas of the crust with Raw Sienna + touch Burnt Sienna. Add more highlights next to these darker tones with the cream mix or cream mix + Yellow Ochre. The "holes" are a dot of cream mix with Raw Sienna for the shadow. The reflected light at the bottom of the bread on the right side next to the basket is Raw Sienna + Burnt Sienna - stroke it up in a curve like the curve of the bread itself. Add an extra shadow on the breadboard under the front and right sides with Burnt Umber.

Reinforce the main highlights on the bread itself with a softened mixture of the cream mix (add a touch of off-white if necessary). Use your mini-fan to stroke over these lightly.

When the bread is dry or almost dry, add a backlight on the lower left corner with the cream or tan mix + Burnt Sienna.

### KNIFE

Paint the blade by reflecting the colors above it onto the shiny surface. Start with the gold mix under the bread; then Raw Sienna from the back edge forward (leaving some of the gold mix); then Burnt Sienna; then a little Burnt Umber on the left side and along the back edge of the blade closer to the handle. Leave it lighter where it meets the shadow of the bread. Add a little cream mix into the front edge.

To the left of the bread reflection, reflect the colors of the basket on the bottle. Start with cream, then shadow it (more on the left) with Raw Sienna and the lavender and purple mixes, then a touch of Burnt Umber. To the left of this, reflect the background colors of lavender and purple with a touch of Alizarin Crimson and/or Viridian in them. This should be darker toward the back or cutting edges of the blade and at the point. Under the stem of the glass add a touch of pale turquoise mix for a reflection of that.

Soften these reflections a bit with the fan brush, then use a flat mock sable brush and purple mix for the lengthwise line just in from the cutting edge. When this line crosses the reflection of the bread, change to Burnt Umber, then Burnt Sienna. Note that it doesn't go all the way to the handle. Blend the "line" slightly towards the cutting edge and soften with the fan brush or mini-fan.

When the knife blade is mostly dry (or dry), add a little extra highlight along the front edge near the tip with the off-white mix.

### KNIFE HANDLE

Paint the top section with Burnt Sienna + touch of Burnt Umber and Liquin. Keep this a little darker along the back edge. Add more Burnt Umber along the side and end. Use Burnt Umber + touch of Burnt Sienna for the bottom section. Soften these a little with your fan or mini-fan. Keep the edge between the top and side soft, not a sharp edge.

Clean out the rivet holes with thinner if necessary. Paint the left one with Yellow Ochre, the middle one with Raw Sienna, and the right one with an orange mix of Cadmium Yellow Medium + touch Grumbacher Red.

Let this all dry a little before you highlight it. Then add a soft highlight along the edge between the top and side (and end) with Raw Sienna. Highlight the corner with the softened pile of cream mix. Brush this to the left and right in a

## Still Life continued

curve around the corner with the mini-fan. Then repeat it, but just barely brush over it this time.

Clean out the channel left for the silver strip of the blade between the top and bottom sections of the handle (use thinner and flat mock sable brush). Notice that this gets a hair wider nearer the end of the handle. When the rest of the knife is dry, paint the edge with lavender and purple mixes, liner brush and thinner. Brush some cream mix into this to reflect the breadboard. Keep the rest of the edge darker until it turns the corner and reflects the green of the grape (see grape directions for colors).

**MIX:**

Orange (1/8 tsp)................Cadmium Yellow Medium + touch Grumbacher Red

### ORANGE

Paint the lower part of the orange inside the basket with the orange mix + Raw Sienna + touch French Ultramarine Blue. Add a little Burnt Sienna on the left and underside. Paint the cast shadow (on right, from grapes) with Burnt Sienna + purple mix. Soften with fan brush leaving the edge of the cast shadow somewhat crisp.

Paint the top part of the orange with the orange mix and Liquin, adding more Cadmium Yellow Medium in the highlight areas (no white yet). Add a touch of Grumbacher Red to some Yellow Ochre for the darker areas; mix Raw Sienna + Grumbacher Red for the darkest shadow areas including the cast shadows. Add a little French Ultramarine Blue to some orange mix for the more grey tones in the shadow areas.

Paint the area inside the basket under the orange with Burnt Umber and a touch of Raw Sienna.

**MIX:**

Lt. Yellow (1/8 tsp) .........................White + Cadmium Yellow Light

Brush some of this into the lightest areas (more will be added later). Add the reflected light on the left side with the gold mix from the bread.

Paint the center "stem" area with lt. yellow mix, then add an accent around it and a dot in the center with liner brush and Raw Sienna + Grumbacher Red.

When the orange is mostly or completely dry, repeat the highlight with the liner brush and light yellow mix (little or no medium). Apply this in a more blotchy pattern, leaving small spots in between strokes. Some strokes should be almost circular. Add some blotchy shapes at the edges of the grayed shadow with the orange mix + French Ultramarine Blue. Add some textured <u>effect</u> within the shadow with the orange mix if necessary.

**MIX:**

Lt. Green (1/4 tsp) ...........................White + Yellow Citron + French Ultramarine Blue
Med. Green (1/8 tsp).........................Lt. Green + Yellow Citron + French Ultramarine Blue + purple mix

### APPLE

Paint the lt. green mix in the green area around the stem. Shadow the right side with the med. green. Bring these greens up further towards the back of the apple than shows in the final picture.

Paint Grumbacher Red + Alizarin Crimson along the top of the apple (+ Liquin) down to the green, but don't blend yet. Start again a little below the green and paint the "front" leaving some space on the right and left for the darker shade. Blend Alizarin Crimson + Viridian into these areas and also into the area below the green, blending down into the Grumbacher Red.

Blend the red and green together at the top of the apple (very gently or the red will take over) bringing the red down in streaks (this is easiest to do when the red and green are a little bit dry). Add more lt. green mix into the red above the green, but leave some darker red along the very top.

When the red on the front of the apple has dried a little, add some lt. green mix and a touch of Cadmium Yellow Medium into the highlight area (this is not the highlight itself, just a "set-up" underneath). Add streaks down the apple with Alizarin Crimson and a chisel edge brush. Be sure not to make these look like stripes.

Brush the entire apple with your fan brush, being careful around the edges and near the green color. Clean any paint off that has streaked over the grapes or oranges. Clean the spot off for the apple stem if it has been painted over.

Highlight the apple when almost dry with the softened pile of off-white mix. Brush over this lightly in both directions with the mini-fan.

**Stem** - Use Burnt Umber (liner brush and thinner) on the left, Burnt Sienna on the right; cream mix + Raw Sienna + Burnt Sienna at the top; highlight with the cream mix.

Reflect the orange color into the apple just above the orange. Soften with fan brush. If this won't show up, wait till the red is a little drier and try again.

### GRAPES

Paint the grapes inside the basket first with the medium green mix, and some purple mix and Burnt Umber where necessary. Shade between the grapes with Viridian + Burnt Sienna + purple mix. Add a darkened shade of the pale turquoise on the under side of some grapes and some orange backlight to the ones closest to the orange.

Put an undercoat of Burnt Umber and thinner (not too thin) on the <u>BASKET</u> before painting the rest of the grapes. Do this only on the tighter weave, not on the more open middle part.

## Still Life continued
### GRAPES continued

Paint  the middle part of each grape with the lt. green mix and Liquin; the upper right side of most with the pale turquoise mixed for the glasses, and the lower left with Yellow Citron.  Blend the medium green mix into the darker areas, adding more purple mix where needed and/or a touch of Burnt Umber.  For grapes that are mostly or all in shadow, darken all or most of them with these darker shades.  Work a <u>little</u> Yellow Ochre into some grapes.

Fill the darker spaces in between grapes with Viridian + Burnt Sienna + a touch med. green or purple mix.  Brush each grape with the corner of the fan brush, but don't over-blend.  Let this dry a little, then reinforce darks if necessary, and clean up the edges with a liner brush.  Outline the stem hole with Raw Sienna, then accent the top of outline with Burnt Umber.  Add a little highlight around the hole in some cases, but be sure not to get it too light.

Highlight the grapes when they have dried a little with the softened pile of off-white mix.  Blur this only slightly with the mini-fan.

**Stems** - Paint with the lt. green mix on the light side, Viridian + Burnt Sienna on the shadow side.  Blend a little with the liner brush.  Add Burnt Umber on the shadow side and in the deeper shadowed areas, then blend again with liner brush.  Repeat the highlight if necessary with the lt. green mix.  Add a backlight on the lower, thicker part of the stem with the pale turquoise mix and French Ultramarine Blue.

### BASKET

When the undercoat is dry, start with the weave along the top rim - Raw Sienna + Burnt Sienna, liner brush and thinner.  Don't worry about shading yet, just draw in the weave with your brush, leaving a little Burnt Umber from the undercoat showing through.  I found it worked best to start from the left and work around to the right.  Where it goes into shadow, use just Burnt Sienna.

After doing the top rim, paint the weave below that, again starting on the left.  Use more Burnt Sienna than Raw Sienna on the left, adding more Raw Sienna as you move to the right.  Note that the "sections" are shorter on the left and more curved.  Also, each strand starts from just under the one to its left.

Let this dry a little, then add some Raw Sienna to the middle of each section of each strand.  Highlight a smaller section with Yellow Ochre, then add a touch of Yellow Ochre and Raw Sienna to the cream mix for a final "dot" of highlight in the middle of these previous highlights.  Use a "dry" liner brush (no paint) to blend the edges of these highlights.  If necessary, go back and add some Burnt Sienna into the left side of each strand in each section (where the strand goes under the previous one).

Paint the  more open strands with Raw Sienna + Burnt Sienna, liner brush and thinner.  Make your mixture darker or lighter (more or less Raw Sienna) as needed to be seen over the fruit.  Add Burnt Umber where the strands are in shadow.  Note that the strands get closer together towards the sides of the basket.  When this dries a little, shadow with Burnt Umber; highlight with Raw Sienna, then the lightest highlight shade mixed for the previous weave.  Pay particular attention to which strand crosses in front of which.

Finish the bottom part of the basket in the same way as the top.  Add a small darker shadow under the basket with Burnt Umber, liner brush and thinner.

Add a final highlight in a few places along the top and on the open weave with White + Cadmium Yellow Medium (not too light).

### WATERDROPS

Follow directions in front of book.  Use Alizarin Crimson for the dark shade on the apple, White + Alizarin Crimson + Grumbacher Red for the light shade. On the orange, use orange mix + Raw Sienna + French Ultramarine Blue (+ Grumbacher Red) for the dark, orange mix + White + Cadmium Yellow Medium for the light. On grapes, add Viridian + Burnt Sienna + lavender to the med. green mix for the dark shade, lt. green + White for the light shade.  Be sure you don't get the dark shades too dark.  Use off-white for the highlights.

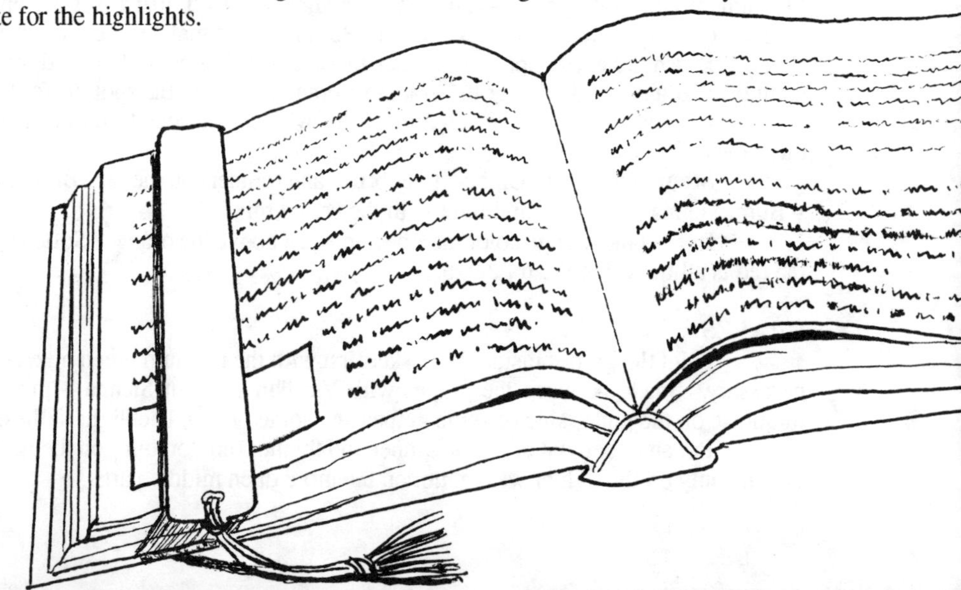

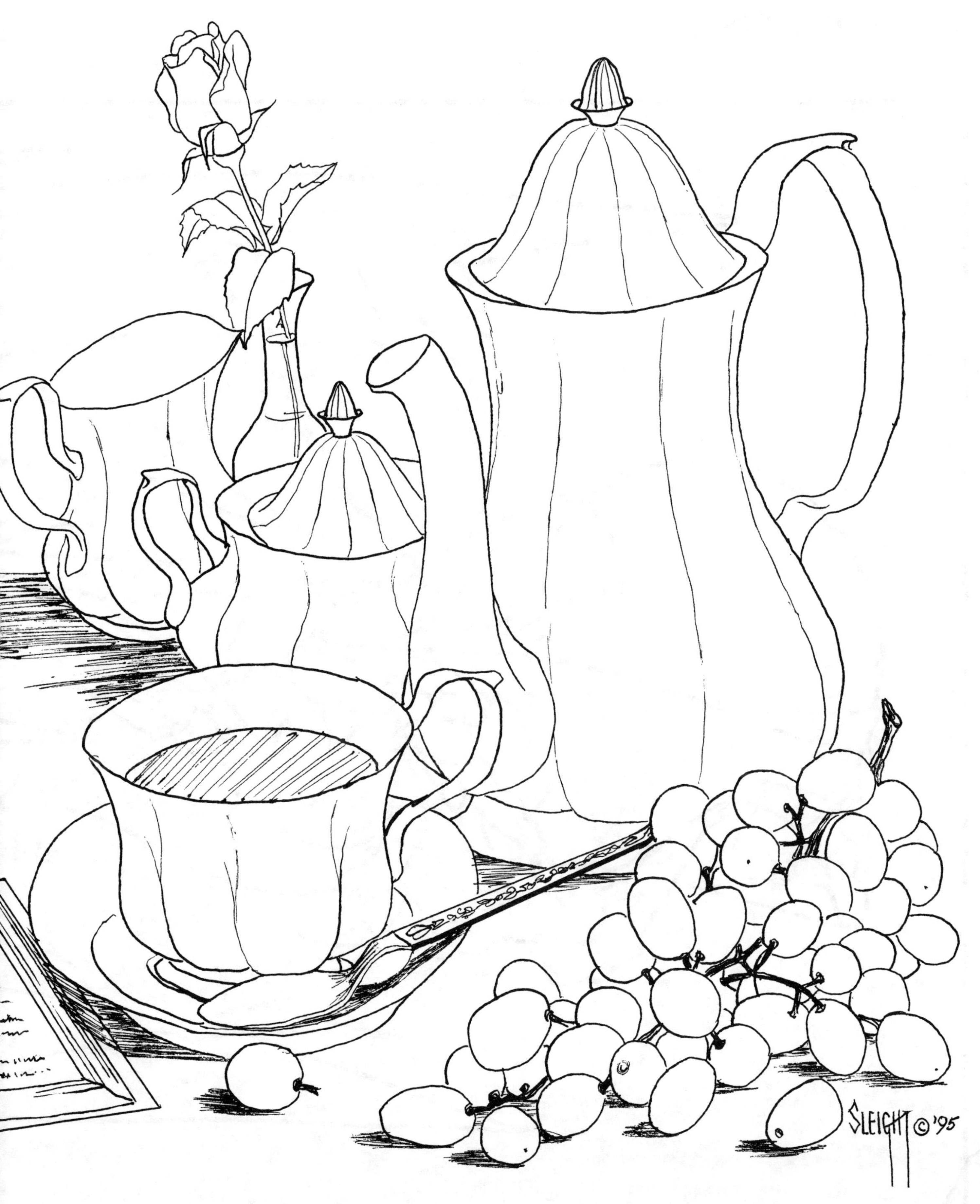

# LAVENDER IRIS

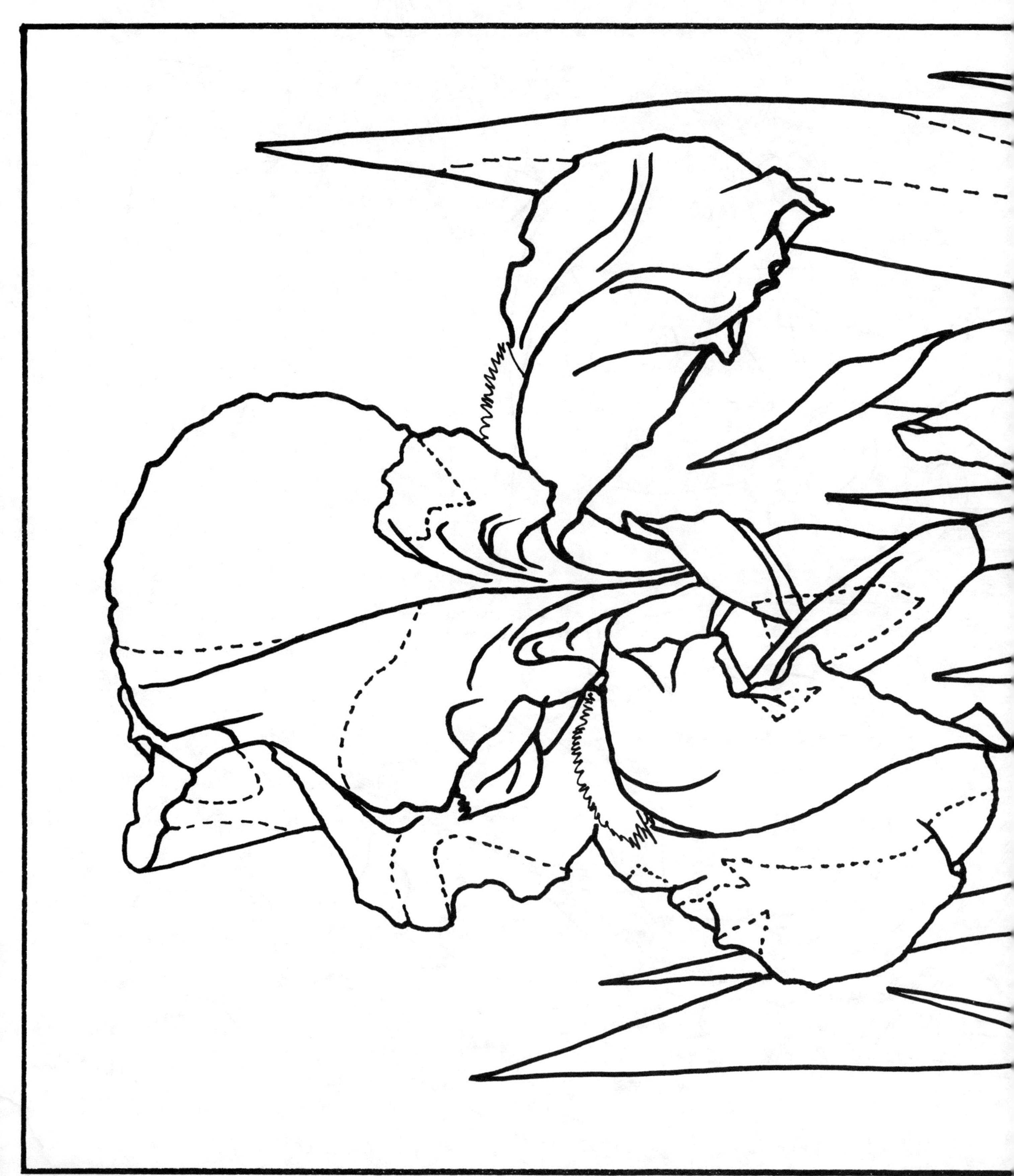

# Lavender Iris on Black

**CANVAS:** 9 x 12 Black

**PALETTE**

| | |
|---|---|
| White | Yellow Citron (Weber) |
| Cadmium Yellow Pale | Leaf Green Medium (Weber) |
| Raw Sienna | Terre Verte (Weber) |
| Grumbacher Red | Burnt Sienna |
| Thalo Red Rose | Burnt Umber |
| French Ultramarine Blue | |

**BRUSHES**
Liner - Preferably Long No. 4
Flat Mock Sables - No. 2 and No. 4 (or equivalent)
Mock Sable Cat's Tongue - No. 4
Small Bristle Fan Brush - No. 2 or No. 3
Optional:  Small Mock Sable Round Brush - No. 3 or No. 4
Sable Fan Brush - No. 2 or No. 3

**MEDIUMS**
Liquin (Winsor & Newton)
Linseed Oil + Thinner (or prepared medium WITHOUT a drier)

**NOTE:**
When working on black or grey canvases, always have a separate container of completely clean thinner to use only when cleaning paint off the background.

**MIX:**
Dk. Green No. 1 (1/4 tsp).......Terre Verte + French Ultramarine Blue
*Dk. Green No. 2 (1/4 tsp).....Leaf Green Medium + French Ultramarine Blue
Med. Green No. 1 (1/4 tsp).....Dk. Green No. 2 + White + Yellow Citron
Med. Green No. 2 (1/4 tsp).....Med. Green No. 1 + White + Yellow Citron
Highlight Green (1/8 tsp)........Med. Green No. 2 + White + Yellow

*Make a larger pile of this mix to start (3/4 tsp) so you can make the light green mixes from it.

Transfer the pattern to your canvas using white transfer paper.

**LEAVES**
Start with the largest leaf on the left.  Use the larger flat mock sable brush, dk. green No. 2 and a touch of Liquin.  Darken the right side a bit with dk. green No. 1; lighten the left side with med. green No. 1.  You can suggest some vertical ridges at this time, but most will be added later.  Brush the leaf vertically with your fan brush (held with bristles vertical), being careful not to brush over the edges.  Ignore the shadows for now, we'll add them when the leaves are dry.

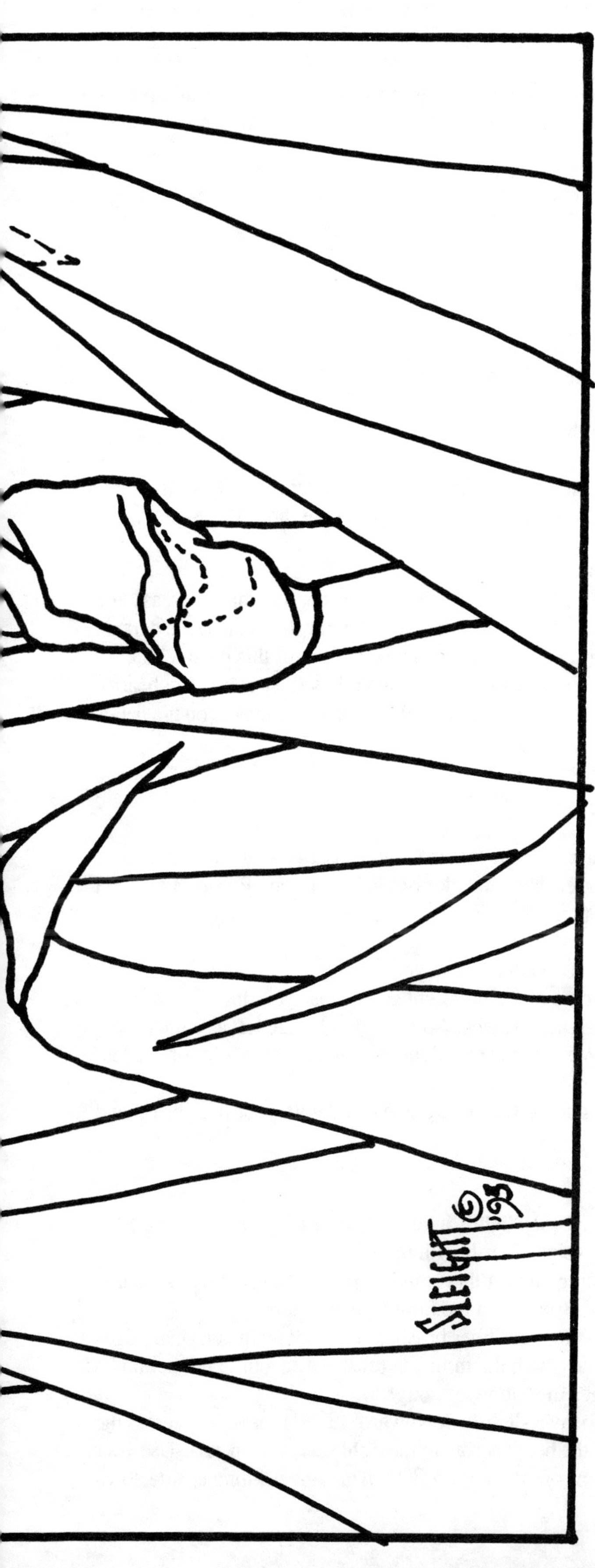

## Lavender Iris on Black continued
### LEAVES continued

Fill in the other two leaves on the left starting with med. green #2 on the top, changing to med. green #1, then dk. green #2 towards the bottom.  *Add some Raw Sienna to the top of the one on the right.  Brush with the fan brush as before.

*Remember to use Liquin when painting in a base coat.  It is usually not necessary to use it in later steps unless the basecoat has gotten too sticky.

Paint the next three leaves to the right in the same amnner, keeping the bigger two darker, the one in the front lighter.  Wait to paint the bent over part of the leaf on the left (or these three) until later when the one behing it is finished.  Brush with the fan brush as before.

**NOTE:** The leaves will not be as light as the finished ones at this stage.

Let the leaves dry a little while you start the iris.

### MIX:

Cream (1/8 tsp) ............................................ White + Cadmium Yellow Pale
*Purple (1/8 tsp)............................................ French Ultramarine Blue + Thalo Red Rose + White
Med. Lavender (1/4 tsp) ............................... Purple + White
Lt. Lavender (1/4 tsp) .................................. Medium Lavender + White
Pale Lavender (1/8 tsp) ................................. Lt. Lavender + White

*Make a larger pile of this mix to start (about 1/2 tsp) so you can make the lighter lavender mixes from it.
**NOTE:**  The upper petals on an iris are called the **STANDARDS** and the lower petals are the **FALLS**.

### IRIS

Start on the left side of the standards with the larger flat mock sable brush (smaller one in smaller areas) and Liquin.  Use the lt. lavender mix in the lighter areas, med. lavender in the darker areas.  Add the purple mix into the darkest areas (note that some areas have a bit more Thalo Red Rose).  Overlap the beard area at the bottom of this petal a bit.

Paint the lower left (fall) petal in the same way, using the cream mix on the shoulders (just below the beard), blending into the lt. lavender below it.  Brush each petal lightly with the fan brush in the direction of the curves on the petals (use corner in small areas).

Let this dry a bit while you go back to the leaves.

### LEAVES

Reinforce the darks (or lights) in the leaves where necessary.  Use the larger flat mock sable with the bristles held vertically to put the ridges on the leaves.  Use a color one shade darker than the color of the leaf it's on.  Be sure you don't space the ridges too evenly.  Some should be closer together than others.

Brush vertically very lightly with your fan brush.

Finish the bent over part of the leaf near the middle if you have not done so yet.

Make a softened pile (see definitions in front of book) of some of the highlight green.  Use your liner brush to put the highlights on the leaves, primarily on the edges except for the brightest leaves.  Some highlights are left as a line, some are blended lightly with the mini-fan (see definitions).  Add a little White to the highlight color for the highlights on the leaf bending over and on the short one in front of it.

If you need highlights on some of the ridges, add some thinner to the med. green No. 2 with your liner brush and use it for these highlights.  Brush very lightly with the mini-fan.

### IRIS

Blend in more med. lavender and purple mix where needed.  Brush lightly again with the fan brush.  Use your liner brush and the purple mix or med. lavender + purple mix to suggest veins.  Brush with mini-fan.

Let this dry a little while you put a base coat and some shading on the other standard petal.  Add a little more Thalo Red Rose to some lt. lavender mix for the areas that are more pink.  Brush with the fan brush as before.

Make a softened pile of some of the pale lavender mix.  Using your liner brush, put this along the brighter edges and into the lightest areas.  Pull this in from the edge where necessary with the mini-fan brush.  Add a little thinner and a touch of Thalo Red Rose to some lt. lavender for highlights on edges in shadow.

Make a softened pile of some of the cream mix.  Use this to lay a slightly downward curved broken line across the lightest area on the shoulder of the left fall (starting at the bottom of the beard across to the right side of the petal).  Use your mini-fan to brush across this in a curve matching the curve of the veins - first downward; then turn the painting upside down and continue the curve toward the beard.

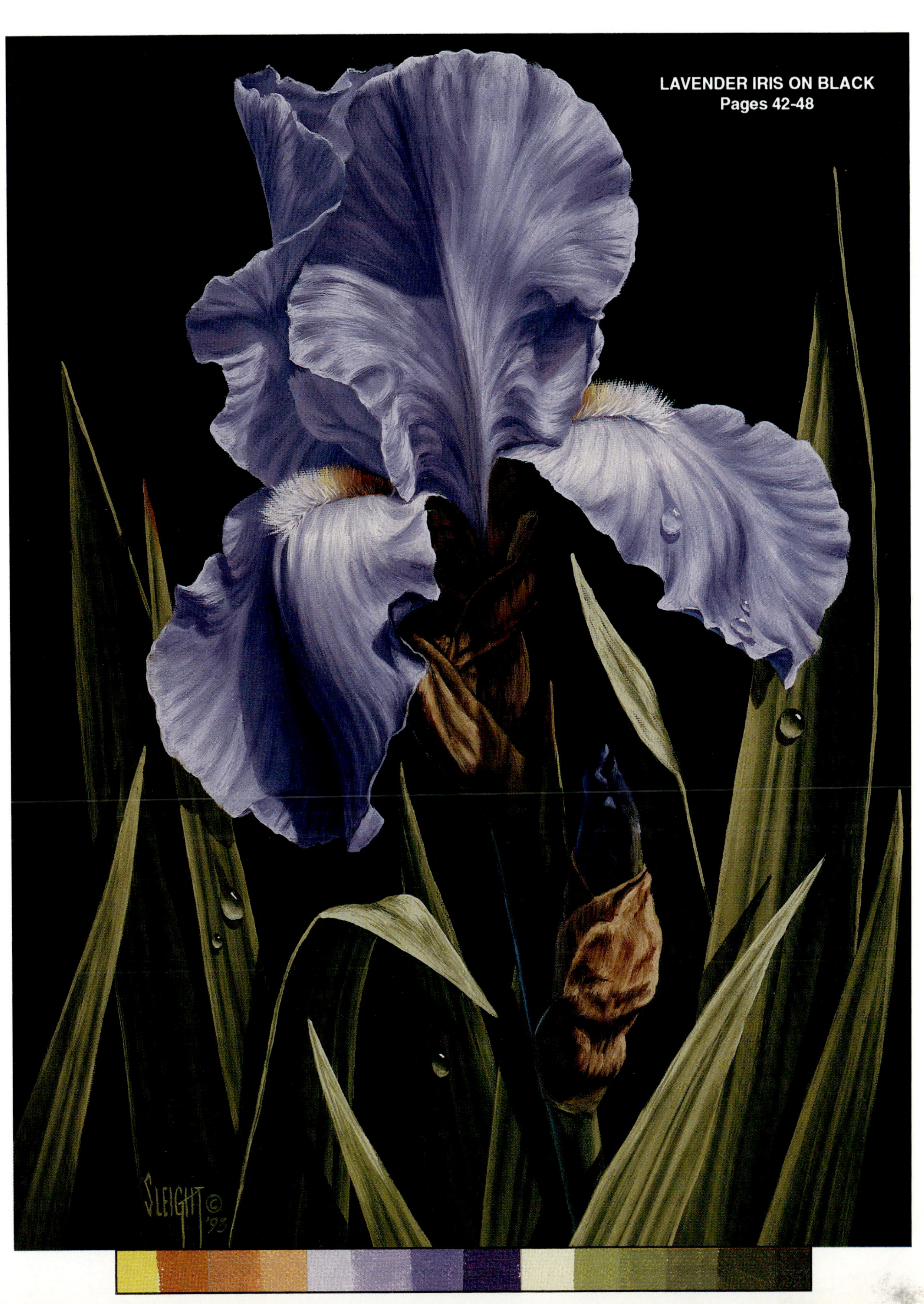

LAVENDER IRIS ON BLACK
Pages 42-48

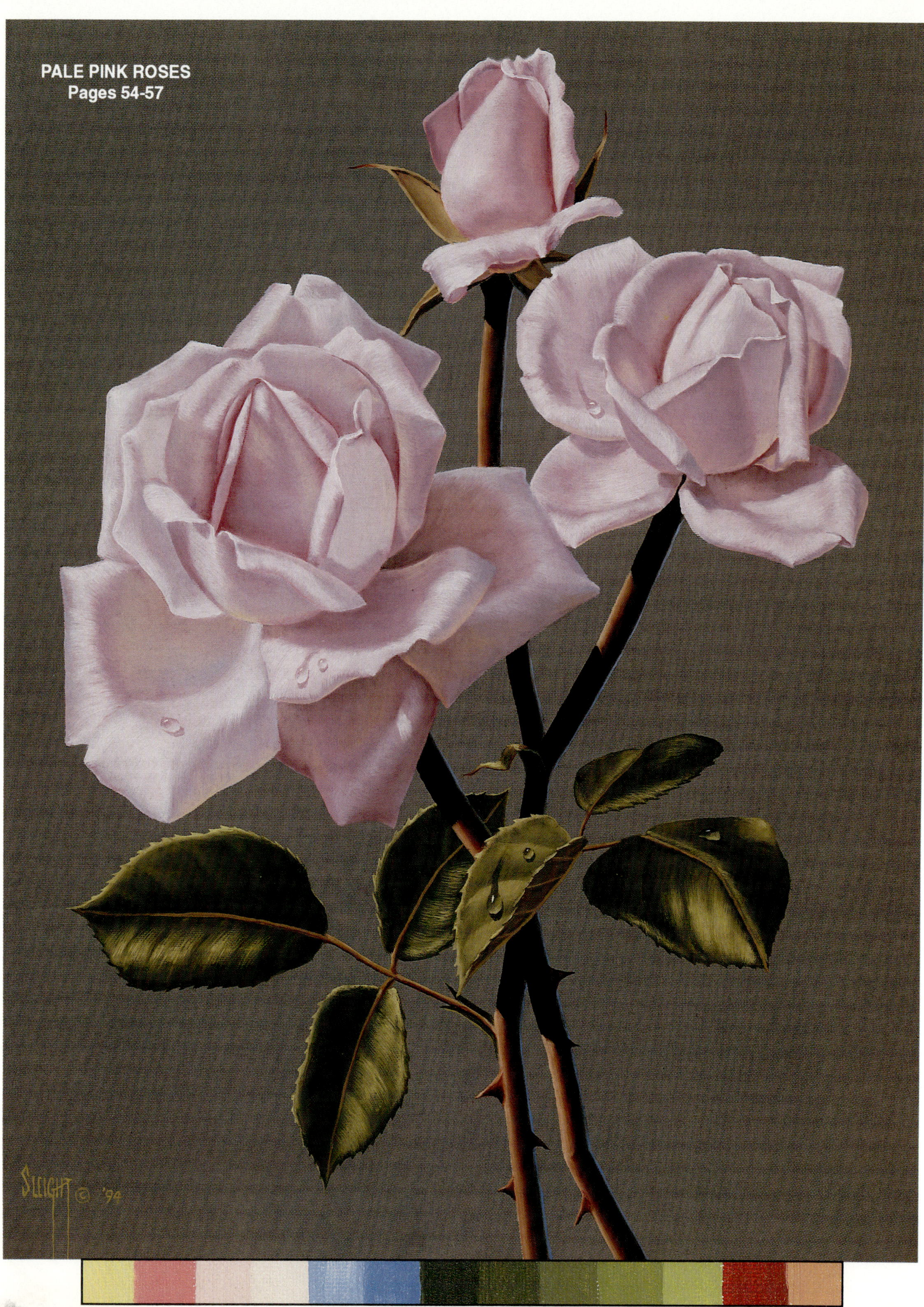

PALE PINK ROSES
Pages 54-57

## Lavender Iris on Black continued

### IRIS continued

Finish the rest of the iris petals in the same way.  The beards will be done later - preferably when the petals are dry.  Suggestion: Paint the tallest leaf on the right before finishing the right fall on the iris.

Paint the underside of the falls (just above the "tissue-like" wrap) with Raw Sienna and Liquin.  Blend some purple mix and some dk. green No. 1 into this.

### MIX:

Lt. Tan (1/8 tsp) ............................. White + Raw Sienna
Tan (1/8 tsp) ................................... White + more Raw Sienna

### "TISSUE-LIKE" WRAP

Fill in the entire "tissue-like" wrap area at the base of the iris with the tan mix, leaving cracks where the lines are.  Use a flat mock sable brush and Liquin.  Add Burnt Umber into this in the shadow areas (smaller flat mock sable or cat's tongue brush), using more Burnt Umber where most of the lines are for more shading.  (Use liner brush there if you want).  Add some Burnt Sienna in the more reddish areas.  Blend some dk. green No. 2 into the area just above the stem.

Brush this lightly with the fan brush (use the corner in smaller places) and let it dry for awhile (work on more leaves or the petal on the right).

When this has gotten to the sticky stage, reinforce the darks, using a liner brush for the finer details.  Brush again with the mini-fan.

Add some highlights in the sunny area with the lt. tan mix and soften with the mini-fan.

Finish the leaf behind the stem before painting the stem.

### STEM

The upper part of the stem is in shadow and therefore painted with dk. green No. 1.  Put a backlight on the left side with a mix of White + French Ultramarine Blue and blend it lightly into the dk. green.  Be sure to get the blue mixture dark enough.  If it looks like a highlight it's too light.  If the backlight disappears onto the green, wait until the green is a little drier, then try again.

The stem below the bud is painted with dk. green No. 1 on the left, then dk. green No. 2, and med. green No. 2 on the right.  Blend the colors together with a dry cat's tongue or small round brush.  Let it dry awhile, then add a brighter highlight with the softened mix of highlight green and a backlight as before.

Finish the next leaf to the right (behind the bud) before painting the bud.

### BUD

Paint the purple part of the bud with the purple mix, changing to dk. green No. 2 in the lower area (use Liquin).

Fill in the "wrap" part of the bud as before with the tan mix, leaving cracks where the lines are.  Shade with Burnt Umber and a little Burnt Sienna as before.  Work a little med. lavender mix into the lighter areas of the bud.  Brush with the fan brush and let it dry awhile.

When it has gotten to the sticky stage, add some lt. lavender in the lightest area of the bud; add a touch of French Ultramarine Blue and Thalo Red Rose to the purple mix for the darkest tones.  Brush a little med. green No. 2 mixed with a touch of the lt. lavender into the lower right area of the bud.

Add more details to the "wrap" area and highlight as before.

### LEAVES

Finish the rest of the leaves as before.  Add some Raw Sienna to the tip of the one nearest the flower.

### MIX:

Gold (1/8 tsp) ................................Cadmium Yellow Pale + Grumbacher Red + purple mix
Lt. Yellow (1/8 tsp) ......................... White + Cadmium Yellow Pale

### BEARDS

**Left Beard:**  Start with the darkest part of the left beard.  Use a liner brush and the gold color for about 1/4 inch.  Keep these short, upward strokes with very little variation in height.  Use a touch of thinner only if necessary.  Clean the brush and change to the lt. yellow mix for another 1/4 inch.  These should gradually get taller.  Clean the brush.

Using a dry brush with upward strokes, stroke back and forth into each color to blend from one into the other.  Fill in the rest of the beard with the cream mix, gradually slanting the strokes more to the left.

Overlap the gold color with a little purple mix starting at the bottom of the strokes, changing to the med. lavender as the color underneath becomes more yellow.  Continue to pull some med. lavender strokes up under the lightest part of the

## Lavender Iris on Black continued
### BEARDS continued

beard, but make these shorter and blend them a little. Overlap these with some more strokes with the lt. yellow mix and then the cream mix, but make these shorter and slanted even more to the left, with just a few very short ones slanted slightly downward. Reinforce the purple shadow at the base of the darker area of the beard.

**Right Beard:** The beard on the right is painted in much the same way, except you start with the lt. yellow mix on the left and blend into the cream mix towards the right (slanting more to the right as you go). Pull a few strokes of the gold mix over the furthest left area of the lt. yellow.

Paint some shorter strokes of med. lavender up under that as before (use lt. lavender under the lightest color), then some more slanted strokes with the cream mix. You can use the softened mix of cream for these last ones, but don't get them too thick. Be sure you have a fairly dark shadow (med lavender + purple) under the beard on the right.

### SHADOWS

When the leaves are dry, paint dk. green No. 1 or No. 2 over the shadow areas depending on how dark the leaf underneath is. If the shadow is painted with dk. green No. 1 add a little dk. green No. 2 where the ridges are; if the shadow is dk. green No. 2, paint some dk, green No. 1 where the dark lines between the ridges are (within the shadow).

Brush lightly with the mini-fan in the shadow area only. Be sure to clean any shadow color off the leaves or background where it doesn't belong (use completely clean thinner when cleaning any paint off the background).

### WATERDROPS

Follow directions in front of book. Be careful not to get the colors too dark.

# Sand Dune

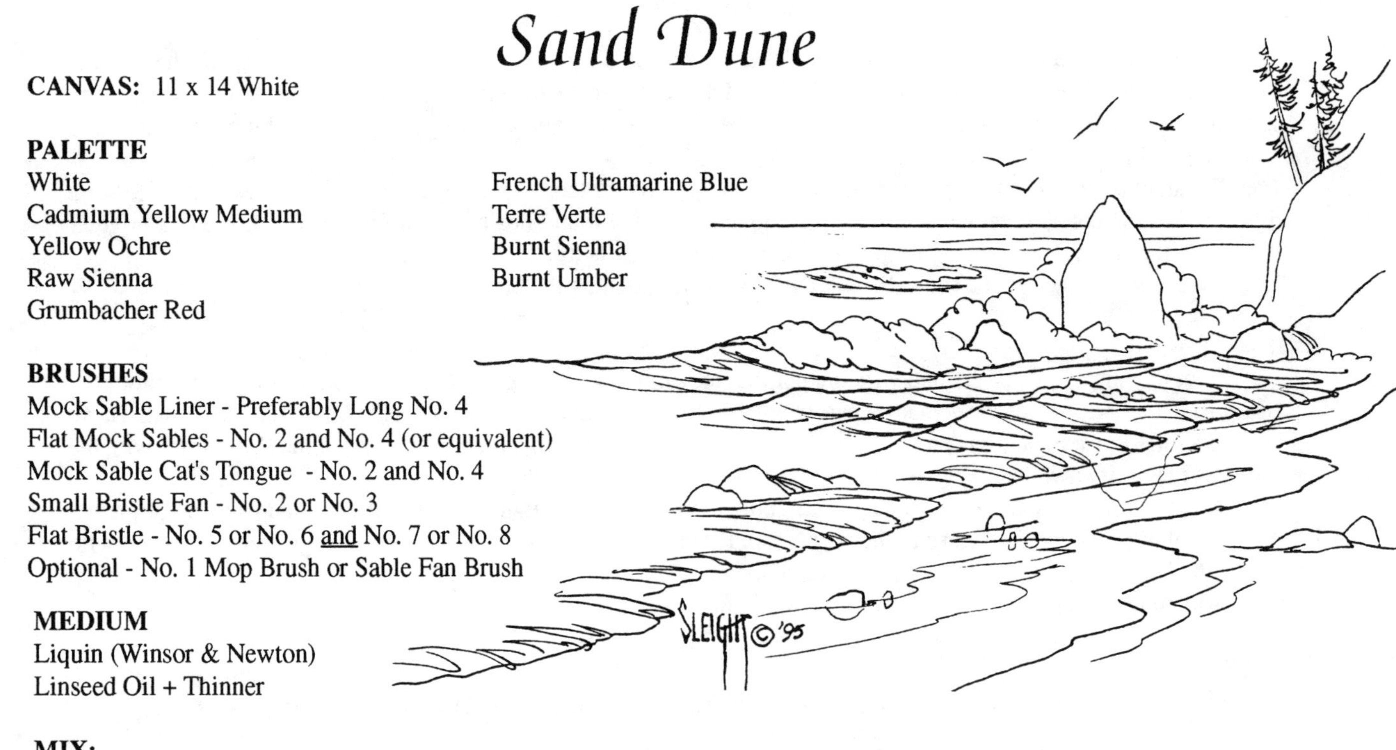


**CANVAS:** 11 x 14 White

**PALETTE**

| | |
|---|---|
| White | French Ultramarine Blue |
| Cadmium Yellow Medium | Terre Verte |
| Yellow Ochre | Burnt Sienna |
| Raw Sienna | Burnt Umber |
| Grumbacher Red | |

**BRUSHES**

Mock Sable Liner - Preferably Long No. 4
Flat Mock Sables - No. 2 and No. 4 (or equivalent)
Mock Sable Cat's Tongue - No. 2 and No. 4
Small Bristle Fan - No. 2 or No. 3
Flat Bristle - No. 5 or No. 6 and No. 7 or No. 8
Optional - No. 1 Mop Brush or Sable Fan Brush

**MEDIUM**

Liquin (Winsor & Newton)
Linseed Oil + Thinner

**MIX:**

Lt. Blue (1/3 tsp) ........................... White + French Ultramarine Blue + touch Cadmium Yellow Medium
*Med. Blue (1/4 tsp) ...................... White + French Ultramarine Blue

*Start with a larger amount of this mix (about 3/4 tsp) so you will have enough to make the deep blue and lavender mixes from it later.

Transfer the pattern to your canvas using graphite paper.

**SKY**

Paint the lt. blue mix in the lower sky from the horizon to about 1-1/2 inch from the top of the canvas. Use a No. 7 or No. 8 flat bristle brush and Liquin. Use med. blue from the top down and blend into the lt. blue.

With your brush, add a touch more French Ultramarine Blue and some Grumbacher Red to a corner of the med. blue (on your palette). Paint this into the top of the sky in the right corner and about 1/2 way across - blend well. Use a fan or mop brush to blend this well. Use criss-cross strokes first, then brush all the sky horizontally.

Let this dry while you put in some of the water. We'll do the clouds when the sky is "sticky".

## Sand Dune continued
**MIX:**

Lavender (1/8 tsp) ............ Med. Blue + French Ultramarine Blue + Grumbacher Red + touch Cadmium
Yellow Medium
Deep Blue (1/4 tsp) .......... Med. Blue + French Ultramarine Blue + lavender mix
Dark Green (1/8 tsp) ........ French Ultramarine Blue + Cadmium Yellow Medium + touch Burnt Sienna
Light Green (1/16 tsp) ...... White + Dk. Green + Cadmium Yellow Medium

### WATER

Paint the deep blue mix all across the horizon and down to the main wave, using the No. 4 flat mock sable brush and Liquin. Add a little of the dark green into this just above the wave and blend it up almost to the horizon (water should be blue at horizon and get greener as it comes closer).

Add some more dark green in horizontal strokes (using chisel edge of same flat brush) for the distant waves. These should be very skinny further away, with one bigger wave closer up. Brush horizontally with fan brush. Keep the top of the distant waves somewhat sharp; blend the bottom into the bluer color.

Paint the lt. green in the transparent area of the wave. Add dk. green in the rest of the wave down to the trough (dotted line) and across under the splashing foam. Blend this into the deep blue and continue down to the "leading edge" of the foam. Drag some of the green down into the deep blue in the form of small wavelets (roughly horizontal, <u>not</u> teepees).

Use the dk. green mix in the "rolling over" area of the main wave.

Brush this with the fan brush, brushing down the wave in a curve like the letter ""C", and horizontally in the water in front of the wave. Brush the transparent area of the wave first, then don't come back to it unless you clean the brush.

Let this dry a bit while you work on the clouds.

**MIX:**

Cream (1/4 tsp) ...............................White + Cadmium Yellow Medium
Pink (1/8 tsp)...................................Cream + touch Grumbacher Red

### CLOUDS

When the sky color is very sticky, but not completely dry, add the clouds.

First use the lavender mix and larger (No. 8) cat's tongue brush to put the curved cirrus-like clouds at the top in (<u>no</u> medium or Liquin, unless the paint underneath is too dry). Start at the top and sweep them around and down to the left, stretching the ends out. Don't forget the slightly more horizontal one behind the right cloud. Put a few strokes a little above the horizon line - these should be very softly blended and horizontal.

With the same brush and the cream mix, put the highlights on these clouds, blending slightly into the lavender. Add a little of the pink mix in between the lavender and the cream and blend slightly.

Use the smaller cat's tongue brush and the cream mix for the light area of the rest of the clouds. Lay the brush slightly on its side and lightly scrub. Don't get it too thick, but it will be thicker than the paint on the sky. Add some of this above the upper clouds too.

Clean the brush and put the shadows on the right and underside of the rest of the clouds with the lavender mix and the cat's tongue brush. Add a few small clouds also.

Clean the brush again and add some pink mix in between the cream and lavender colors. Blend lightly with the cat's tongue.

Use a mop brush or a sable fan brush to soften the clouds. For the cirrus clouds at the top, brush with the curve, then very lightly horizontally. Use a very light "X" stroke over the rest of the clouds, then brush horizontally.

**MIX:**

Tan (1/2 tsp) .....................White + Burnt Umber

### WATER

Add some highlights or "caps" on top of the distant waves. Use a liner brush, thinner and the light blue mix. Add some strokes on the flat water between the waves with the medium blue mix and the lavender mix.

Paint the dk. green mix in the top part of the "rolling-over" area of the main wave. Add a little thinner to some lt. blue mix. With your liner brush, lay a semi-thick line across the top of the dk. green (not too thick). Make a mini-fan out of your long liner (See Defintions). With this, stroke across the line and down to the right in an arc - very lightly. If you cover up all the green, you used too much lt. blue paint! Wipe it off and try again.

## Sand Dune continued
### FOAM ON THE WATER

Add a little more blue and a <u>touch</u> of red (not enough to make it lavender) to a corner of the deep blue. Fill in the splashing and blowing foam with this, leaving a little space at the top for the highlight. Keep this relatively thin - no ridges of thick paint. Tap some cream mix in the space left (add a little thinner) - either with your liner brush or another small brush (an older flat mock sable or cat's tongue works well). This should be a bit thicker than the blue. Blend it into the blue below it by tapping with a dry brush. Make a mini-fan out of your liner and use it to pull the top (highlight) up to the left, like it's blowing in the wind. Add an irregular line along the top of the rest of the wave on the left with the cream mix (liner brush and a little thinner).

### FOAM PATTERNS

Use the deep blue mix (mix a little thinner into it) on the face of the wave, a liner brush and thinner. Stroke up into the wave, or down from the top, whichever works best for you, in slightly curved, zig-zag strokes with some roughly oval shapes. Where there are lines, make some of them thick (press harder on the brush), some thin or irregular (less pressure).

With the liner brush, thinner and the medium blue, put some foam on the flat water. These should be more horizontal strokes - especially along the top of the wavelet in front of the main wave.

Use the mini-fan brush (made from your liner) to soften the foam patterns a bit. Brush up into the wave or down from the top.

Put a rather thick line of cream mix along the leading edge of the foam "line" below the main wave. There are two ways to do this:

1. Add some thinner to some cream mix and use a liner brush to put it on.
2. Load some cream mix on one side of the No. 4 flat mock sable brush. This should be a thick

ridge at the end of the bristles. Hold the brush with the bristles horizontal and the paint on the underside. Stroke the brush horizontally following the edge of the foam, leaving a lip of paint as you go.

Stroke this lightly back into the water behind it.

### WATER

Fill in the next section of water with deep blue + light blue under the previous "ripple", blending down into lt. blue to the next line. Add a little lavender mix and pink mix in vertical strokes down through this for color variation.

### SAND

Fill in the entire flat sand area (not the dune) with the tan mix and a little Liquin. Add a touch more Burnt Umber close to the water, some lavender mix here and there in the rest. Brush the deeper tan area right into the water, carrying some of it well into the blue. Brush all of this horizontally with the fan brush.

### WATER

Add a shadow beneath the previous "ripple" with the deep blue + French Ultramarine Blue + a touch of dk. green (don't turn it green). Use a liner brush and thinner. Soften this just a bit with the mini-fan.

Paint the next ripple in the same way as previous. Stroke it lightly back toward the previous ripple using the mini-fan or a sable fan brush; Add a few zig-zag foam pattern-like strokes with the liner brush and cream mix. Shadow under each ripple as before, but with a little lighter shade of blue/green. Soften a bit with mini-fan or sable fan.

### GRASS

Start on the left side at the top of the dune (or on the right if you are left handed). Use a No. 5 or No. 6 flat bristle brush held with the bristles vertical (use the "chisel" edge) and Raw Sienna. Fill in the solid space in the lower middle of each clump of grass, then stroke upward in a slight curve while pulling the brush away from the canvas. Don't try to put every blade of grass in - we'll do more with a liner brush after this. Add some Burnt Umber over the bottom and middle area.

Work some thinner into some Raw Sienna with your brush. This should be very fluid, but not runny. Be sure there's enough paint mixed in evenly. Clean the brush and roll the bristles on your rag to form a good point. Put some individual grasses in around the top of the clump. Try to keep your hand moving while you do these - don't be too deliberate - they tend to get too thick then. Put very little pressure on the brush (so only the tip touches the canvas) and pull your hand away from the canvas at the top of each blade. These strokes don't all need to start at the bottom. Pull a few out further to put "seeds" on later.

Overlap these with some strokes of Yellow Ochre in the same way. Also add a few strokes with the dark green mix.

## Sand Dune continued
### GRASS continued

Mix two lighter shades of White + Yellow Ochre.  The lighter one should be darker than your cream mix.  Add some strokes first with the darker of these (add thinner as before).  If these don't show up well, let it dry a little while you work on other clumps or on the sand.  Then try again.  Finish with the lighter color grasses, some of which curve sharper and are closer to the ground.

### SAND

Paint the top left clump of grass, then put the sand in below it.  Add a little Burnt Sienna and some White to your tan mix (to make it lighter and brighter).  Use this for the sand (add Liquin) - shading it with Burnt Umber and with the deep blue mix.  Add the grasses in front of this clump (use liner brush and lighter colors), then put the shadows on the sand with Burnt Umber (liner brush and thinner).

Next, paint the next clump of grass to the right in the same way as before; then the sand below it and the individual grasses below it, etc.

At this point you could put in the rest of the sand if you will be able to finish it at this sitting.  If not, just paint it in below the grass on the left for now.  The shading in the sand must be done while it's wet. Lighten the sand in the middle with the lightest Yellow Ochre + White mix.  Darken it at the bottom and corners with Burnt Umber and some of the deep blue mix.  To make the ripples in the sand, use the chisel edge of the No. 4 flat mock sable brush and Burnt Umber + deep blue mixed together.

### TIPS FOR GRASSES
1.      Practice them on your palette first.
2.      They're generally easier or at least less scary if done over a dry sky.  At least they can be
        removed then if you get one too thick!
3.      For the seed or grains at the top of some, use a liner brush with the bristles flattened out
        a bit (not as far as a fan).  Use tapping strokes, first with Burnt Sienna, then Raw Sienna,
        then Yellow Ochre (working to the left).  A few have a touch of the darker mix of Yellow
        Ochre + White.
4.      Use  lighter green  strokes in some of the grasses (mix dk. green + Cadmium Yellow Medium).
5.      On the right side, most of the shadows go up the hill except where the grasses are bent over to
        the left near the ground.

### DRIFTWOOD

Paint the driftwood and its shadows with Burnt Umber and thinner. Don't get this too thin - canvas should not show through.  After this has dried a little (should be sticky, but not dry), add the bark with your No. 4 flat mock sable brush.  Add some Burnt Sienna and Burnt Umber to some of the tan mix that you used for the sand and make lengthwise strokes, stopping where there's a shadow.  Don't leave too much space between the strokes, just cracks except where there's a shadow area.

Mix White + Burnt Sienna - quite light - for the highlights.  If this picks up too much of the undercoat, let it dry a bit and try again.  You may need to use your liner brush for the highlights. Blend the edges of the highlights slightly into the mid-tone color you put on first.

Add a backlight with the deep blue + more French Ultramarine Blue on the underside of the driftwood (separating it from its shadow).  Use your No. 4 flat mock sable for this so it will blend slightly into the Burnt Umber.

The driftwood on the right is painted in the same way, except there's a bit more highlight.  The one on the left is much smaller so there are fewer strokes and details.

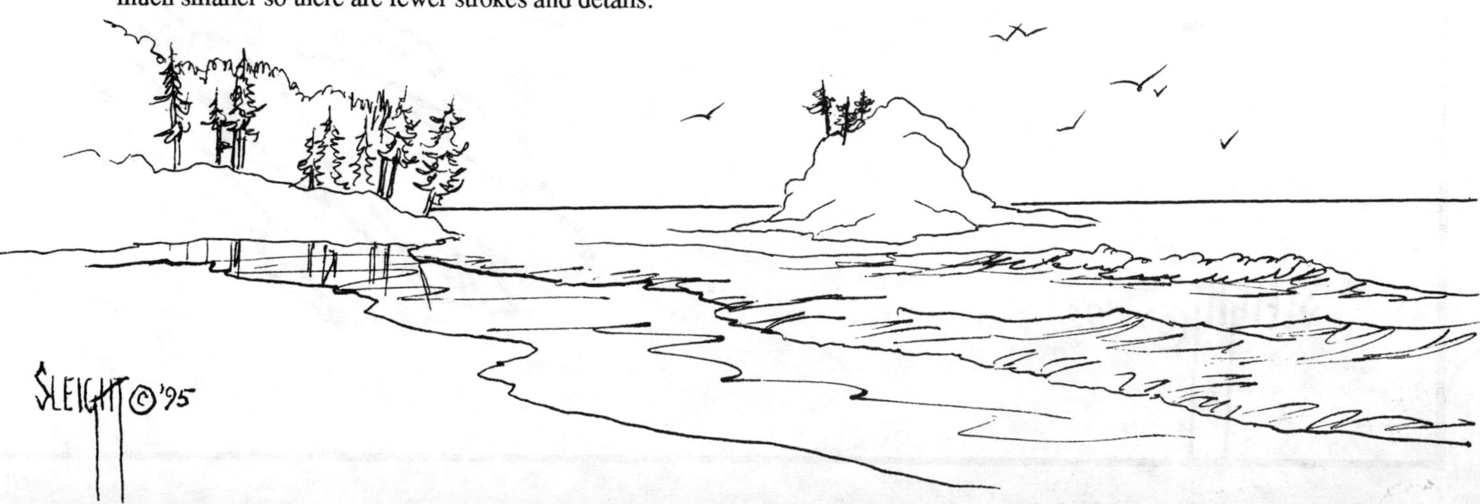

# SAND DUNE

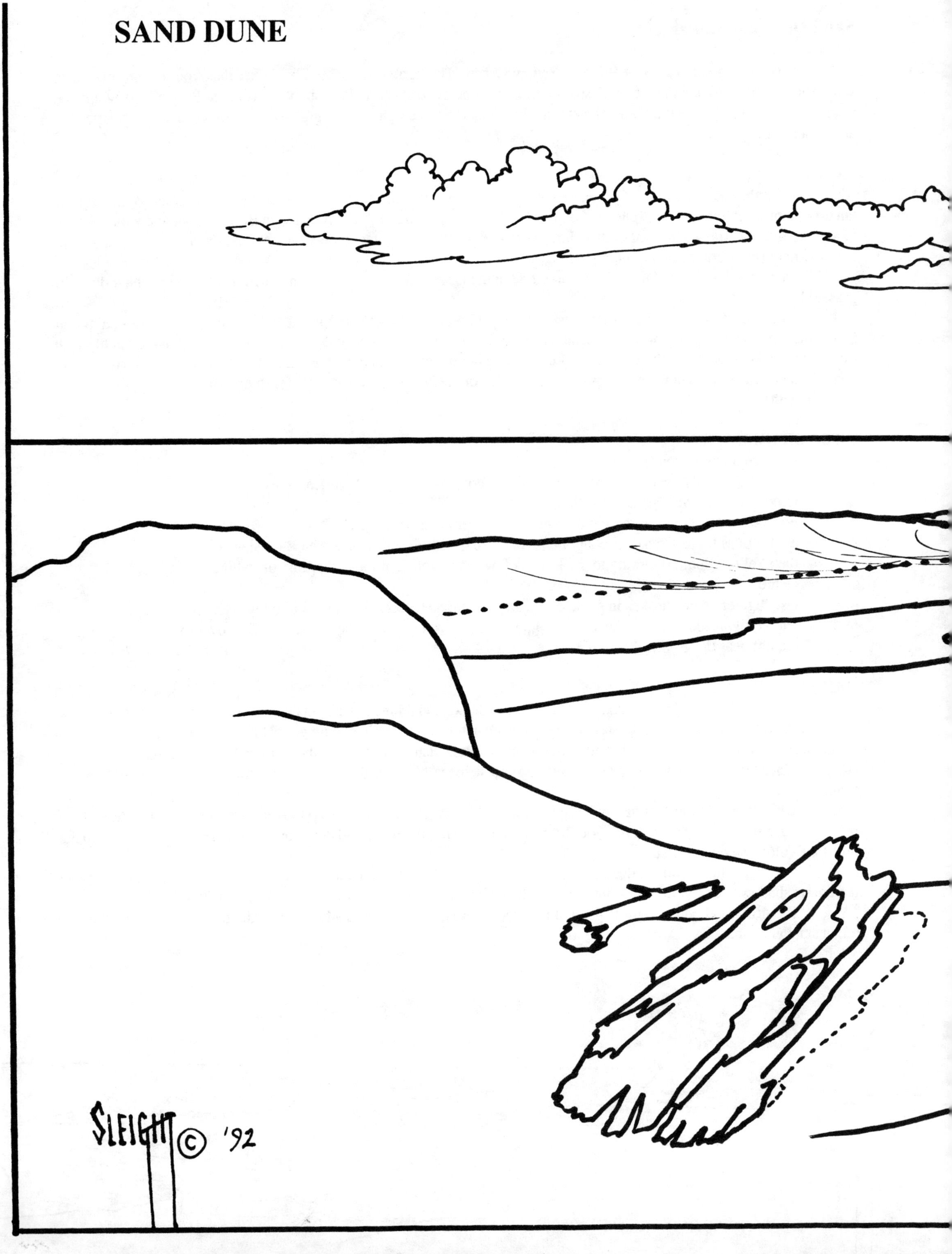

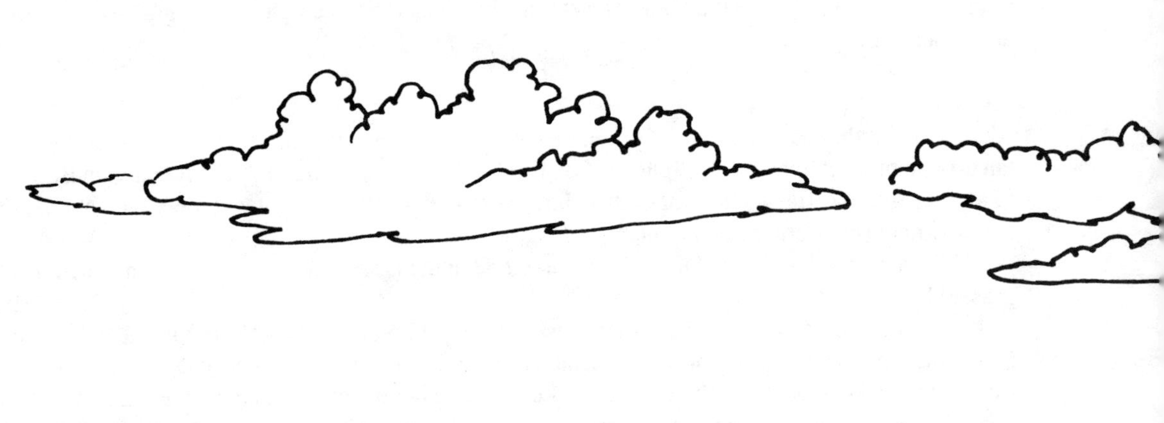

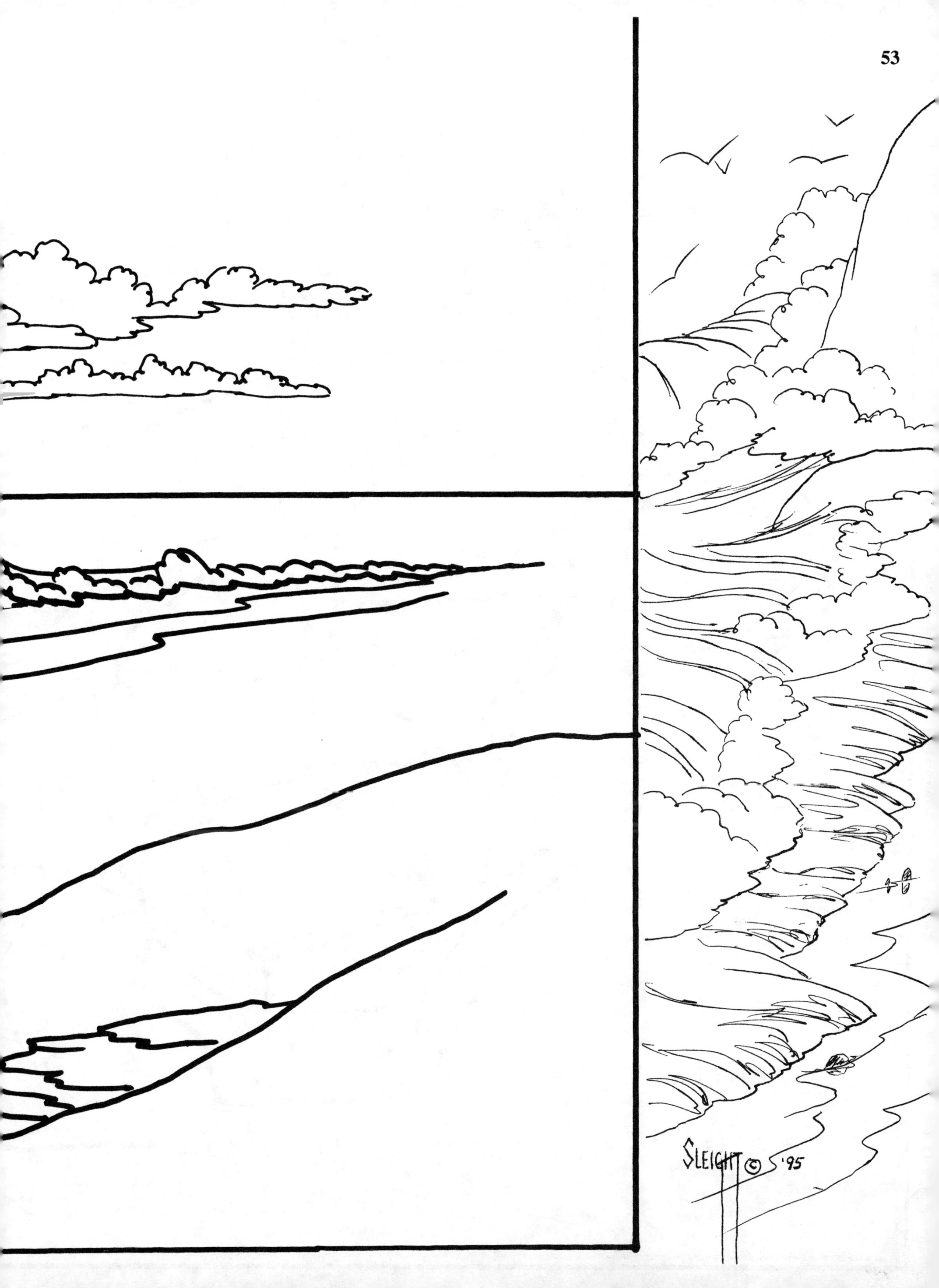
SLEIGHT © '95

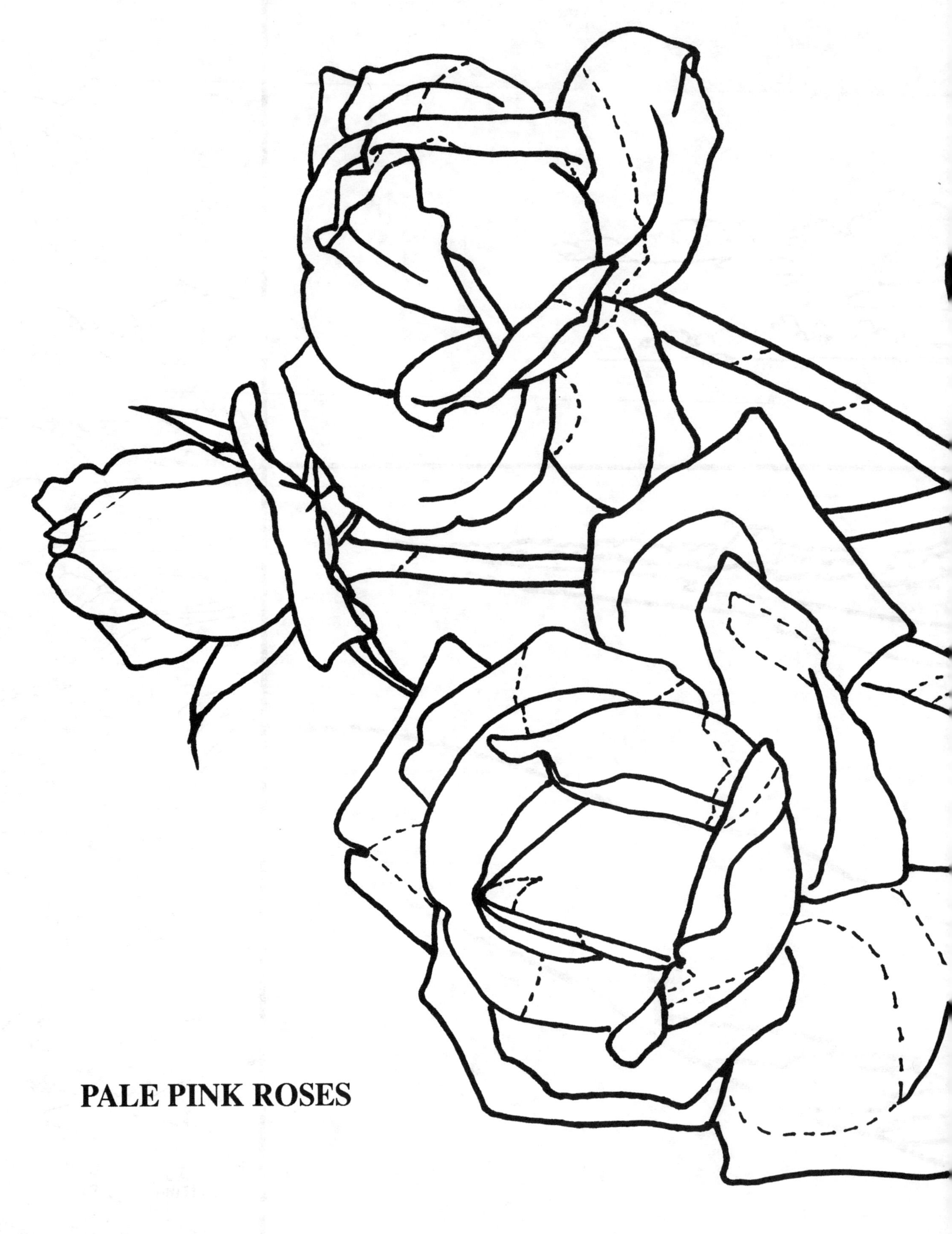


PALE PINK ROSES

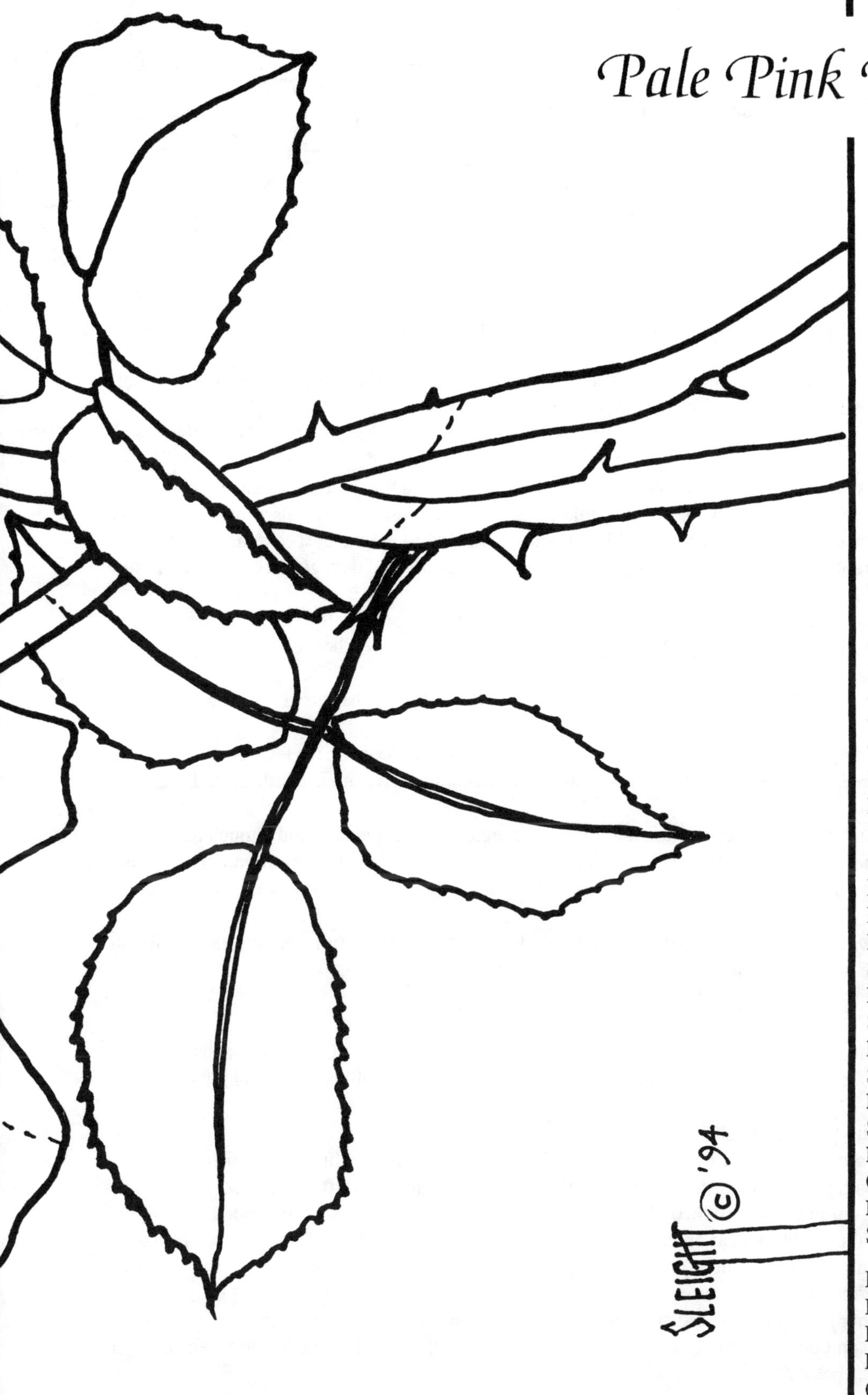


# Pale Pink Roses on Grey

**CANVAS:** 11 X 14 Grey

If you decide not to use the Dream Canvas (which comes in grey) for this painting, you will need to paint a white canvas with grey <u>acrylic</u> paint. I would suggest any of the following mixtures: (Acrylics)

White + Ultramarine Blue + Burnt Sienna
White + Ivory Black + touch of Ultramarine Blue
White + Paynes Grey + touch Burnt Sienna

**PALETTE**
White
Yellow Citron (Weber)
Cadmium Yellow Light
Leaf Green Medium (Weber)
Grumbacher Red
Terre Verte (Weber)
Thalo Red Rose
Burnt Sienna
French Ultramarine Blue
Burnt Umber

**BRUSHES**
Liner (preferably long) -
No. 4
Small Flat Mock Sables -
No. 2 and No. 4 (or equivalent)
Small Cat's Tongue Brush -
No. 4
Small Round Mock Sable -
No. 4
Small Bristle Fan Brush -
No. 2 or No. 3
Optional -
No. 3 or No. 4
Sable Fan Brush

**MEDIUMS**
Linseed Oil + Thinner or
Prepared Medium without drier
Liquin -
(Winsor & Newton product)

## Pale Pink Roses on Grey continued

**MIX:**

| | |
|---|---|
| Cream (1/8 tsp) | White + Cadmium Yellow Light |
| Medium Pink (1/2 tsp) | White + Grumbacher Red + touch of Thalo Red Rose |
| Light Pink (1/2 tsp) | White + Medium Pink |
| Highlight Pink (1/8 tsp) | White + Medium Pink |
| Light Blue (1/4 tsp) | White + French Ultramarine Blue |
| Medium Blue (1/8 tsp) | White + more French Ultramarine Blue |
| Dk. Green No. 1 (1/4 tsp) | Terre Verte + French Ultramarine Blue |
| *Dk. Green No. 2 (1/8 tsp) | Leaf Green Medium + French Ultramarine Blue |
| Medium Green No. 1 (1/4 tsp) | Dk. Green No. 2 + White + Yellow Citron |
| Medium Green No. 2 (1/4 tsp) | Medium Green No. 1 + White + Yellow Citron |
| Highlight Green (1/8 tsp) | Medium Green No. 2 + White + Yellow Citron |
| Red (1/8 tsp) | Grumbacher Red + Thalo Red Rose + Dk. Green No. 1 |
| Tan (1/8 tsp) | White + Burnt Sienna |

*Make a large pile of this to start (1 tsp) so you can make the lighter green mixes from it.

Transfer the pattern to the canvas using white or black transfer paper depending on shade of canvas. Use a soft eraser to remove any white or black that does not belong to the pattern.

### TOP BUD

Fill in the two small petals on the left with medium pink, Liquin and a small flat brush. Use the same color for the right side of the middle (largest) petal. Paint the other side of the middle petal and the rest of the petals with the light pink mix, leaving small cracks where the lines are. Use little or no Liquin with the lt. pink to get the best coverage. If the light pink doesn't cover the grey canvas sufficiently without getting too thick, let it dry a little and then go back later with a cat's tongue brush and a second coat of lt. pink.

Blend the light and medium pinks together down the middle of the large middle petal with your cat's tongue brush. Add a little medium blue and medium pink into the shadow areas. The cat's tongue works well here because you can blend the colors at the same time.

Brush each petal very lightly with the fan brush (bristle or sable) to even out the brush strokes and blend a little.

### LARGER ROSE

Let the top bud dry a little while you put a base coat on the left side of the larger bloom on the left. Use lt. pink only here at first since this flower is considerably lighter; leave cracks for the lines as before. Again, use little or no Liquin for the best coverage.

Blend medium pink and light and/or medium blue into the darker areas of these petals. Add a touch more Cadmium Yellow Light to some of the cream mix and work it into the more yellow spots. Don't worry if you can't get the shadow areas dark enough yet. We'll come back later when it's more dry and put those in (and also some brighter highlights).

Brush each petal lightly with the fan brush (bristle or sable). Use just the corner of the brush in small areas. Brush in the direction the veins would be growing if you could see them.

### TOP BUD

Go back to the top bud and add some deeper shadows with medium pink and lt. or med. blue, then add a little red mix for even deeper tones. Use the smaller flat mock sable or cat's tongue brush, then the small round brush for the smallest areas.

Brush the petals again with your fan brush.

Add some final darker accents with your liner brush, med. pink + red mix + med. blue and a touch of thinner. Brush these accents very lightly with your liner brush made into a mini-fan (See definition in front of book).

Make a softened pile (see definitions) of some of the highlight pink mix. Using your liner brush, put a bead of this along the highlight areas (look for the brightest areas on the rose). The thickness depends on the area to be highlighted - the smaller areas will need much less highlight. The highlight on the larger middle petal goes horizontally across the light area only, and about 1/3 above the bottom with a slight curve.

Make a mini-fan out of your liner again and brush lightly across the bead of highlight - usually in a curve. Turn the painting sideways or upside down and pull the paint in the opposite direction. Note, highlights that are along an edge get brushed one direction only (into the petal).

## Pale Pink Roses on Grey continued

### CALYXES ON BUD

Add Burnt Sienna to the highlight green for the lighter areas.  Use a  small brush and Liquin.  Shade with Burnt Sienna and the med. green mixes, then the darker greens and Burnt Sienna for the darkest areas.  Highlight the edges with highlight green + Burnt Sienna and White or the cream mix.  Add just a touch of Burnt Sienna at the ends of the calyxes (use liner brush and thinner).

### LARGER ROSE

Go back to the larger blossom and but a base coat and a little shading on several more petals.  Brush with the fan brush as before.

Add more dark shading on the left side of this rose with med. pink + light and/or med. blue, and then with some red mix added.  Reinforce the yellower areas where necessary.

Add highlights as you did on the bud.

Continue through the blossom on the left - putting a base coat and some shading on several petals while others are drying a bit.  Go back to previous petals and add more shading with med. pink, lt. and med. blues, and the red mix, also adding a little yellow or yellow + white where necessary.  Brush with a fan brush, then highlight with a liner and the softened mix of highlight pink, brushing over the highlight with the mini-fan.

For the darker petals on the right and bottom sides, add some dk. green No. 1 into the darker areas (after adding a little more red mix).

Put a "backlight" on the bottom side of some petals with the cream mix + med. pink mix - sometimes adding a touch more Cadmium Yellow Light.  Brush this slightly into the petal with the mini-fan.

**ROSE ON RIGHT:**  Paint in the same way as the other two.

### STEMS

Paint Burnt Umber in the shadow areas and down the right side in the light areas (use Liquin and small brush).  Use Burnt Sienna down the middle, and the tan mix down the left side.  Blend with a cat's tongue brush or a fan brush stroking vertically.  Add a  little med. green No. 1 down the middle.

Repeat the highlight down the left side with a liner brush and the tan mix (add a touch of thinner).  Add a little more French Ultramarine Blue to some med. blue mix for a backlight down the right side of the stems, applying it with a liner brush and a touch of thinner.

### LEAVES

Paint the left three leaves with dk. green #2 in the darker areas, med. green No. 1 for the middle tones, med. green No. 2 in the lightest areas, leaving a crack where the center vein is.  Use the larger flat mock sable brush and Liquin.  Add some dk. green No. 1 into the dk. green No. 2 in the darkest areas.

Brush each leaf with the fan brush, brushing from the center out, or from outside edges in.  Let them dry a bit, then put in the "veins" on each side (not middle) with a cat's tongue and one shade darker than the base coat in each area.  Use the corner of the larger flat mock sable brush for the "teeth" along the edges.  Be sure to make these little triangles and not just "hairs.

Brush again with the fan brush in the same way as before; then brush lightly <u>lengthwise</u> across the "veins" to blur them a little (this avoids the striped look).  Finally, brush again from the center out or from outside edges in.

Add some Burnt Sienna to some med. green No. 2 for the vein down the middle - use a liner brush and thinner.

Highlight the leaves with a softened mixture of the highlight green in the same way you did the flowers.  Don't get the highlight along the edges too thick.  Pull it just slightly into each leaf with the mini-fan.

Paint the leaves on the right in the same way.  Add a little Burnt Sienna to some med. green No. 1 for the underside of the leaf in front of the stems.  Form the veins in it with Burnt Sienna + med. green No. 2.

### THORNS

Fill the thorns in with Burnt Sienna, shadowing the underside with Burnt Umber.  Highlight the top side with the tan mix used to highlight the stems.

### WATERDROPS

Follow directions in front of book.  Be careful not to get the colors too dark.

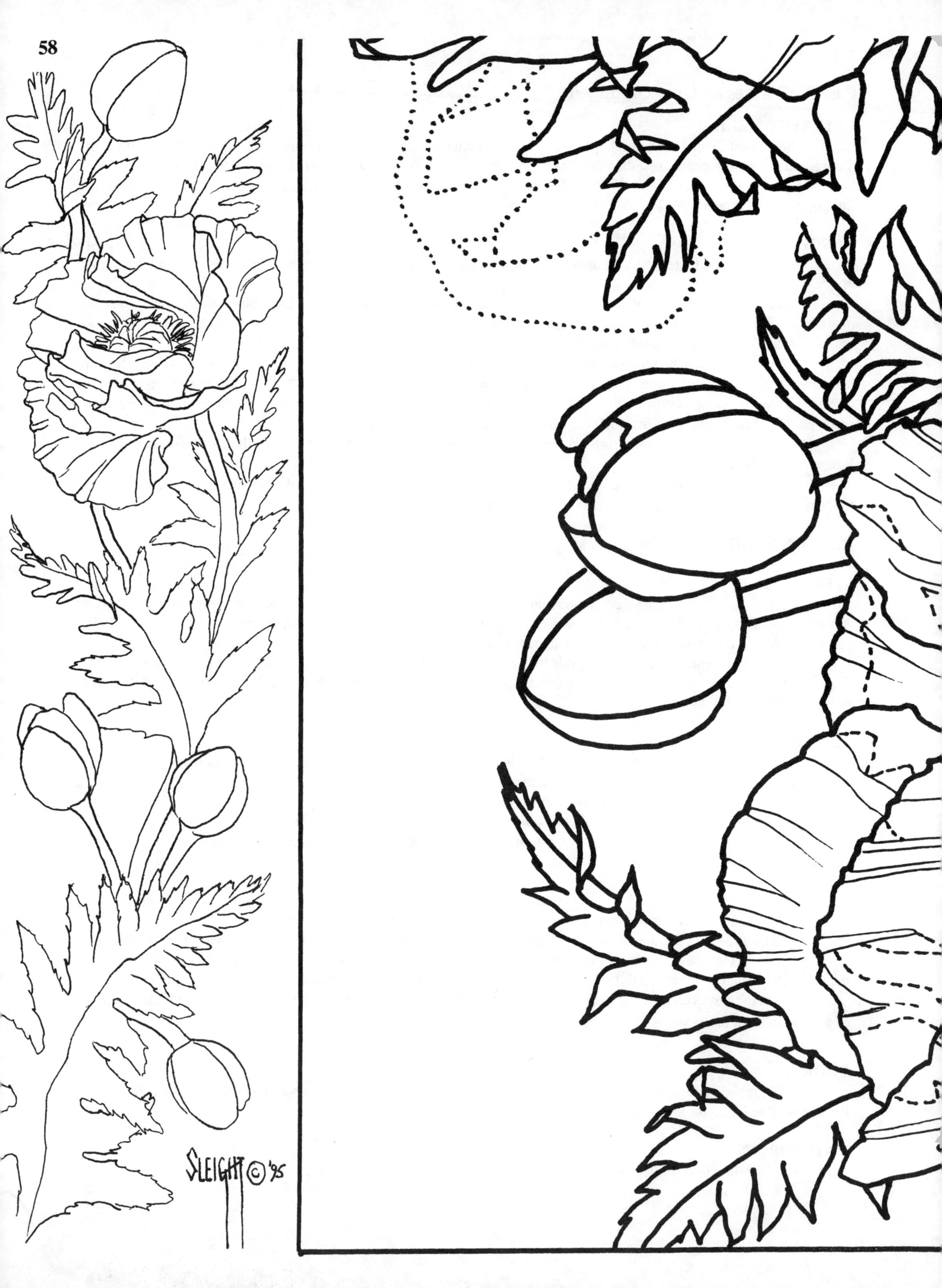
58
SLEIGHT ©'95

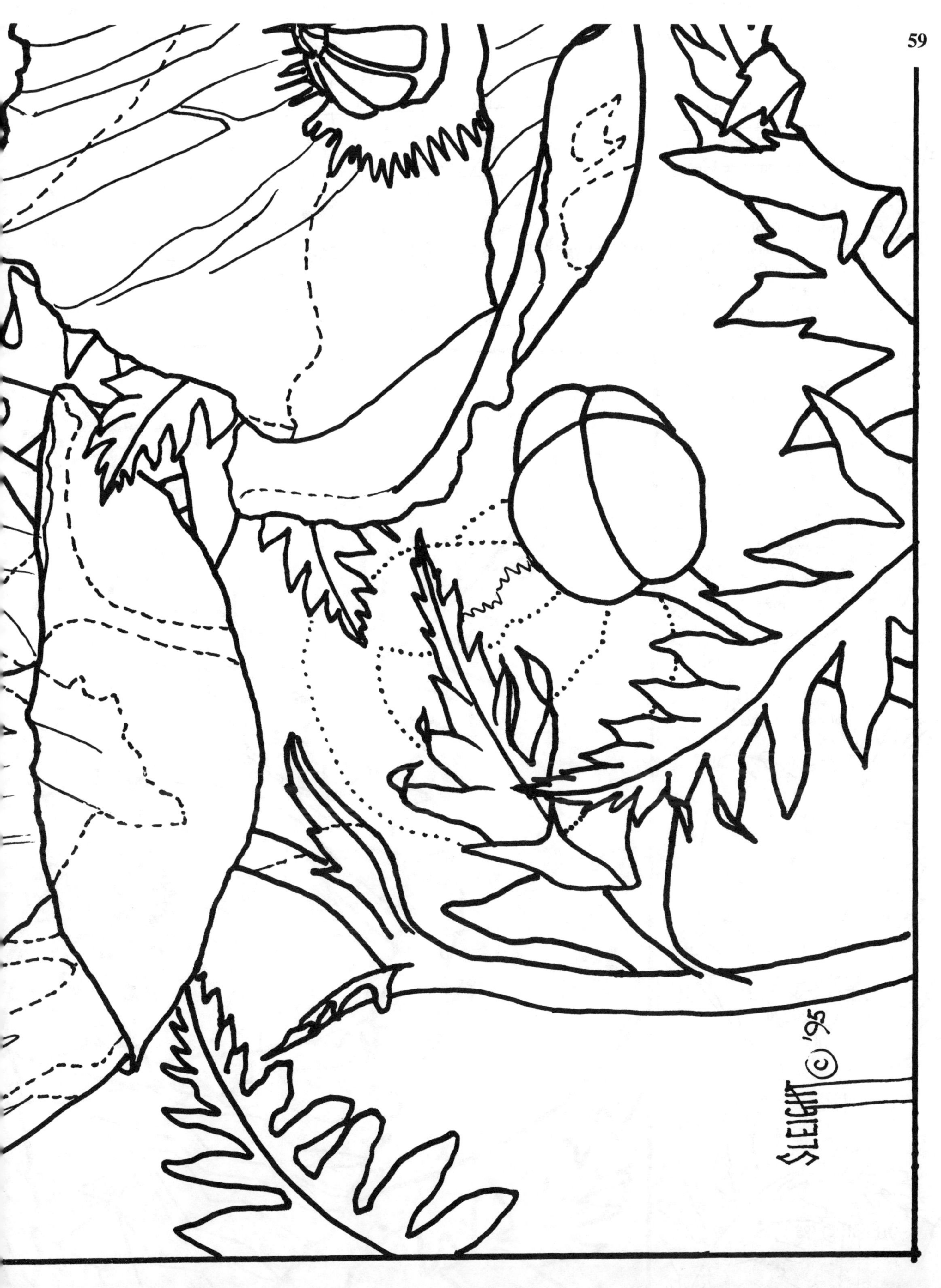
SLEIGHT © '95

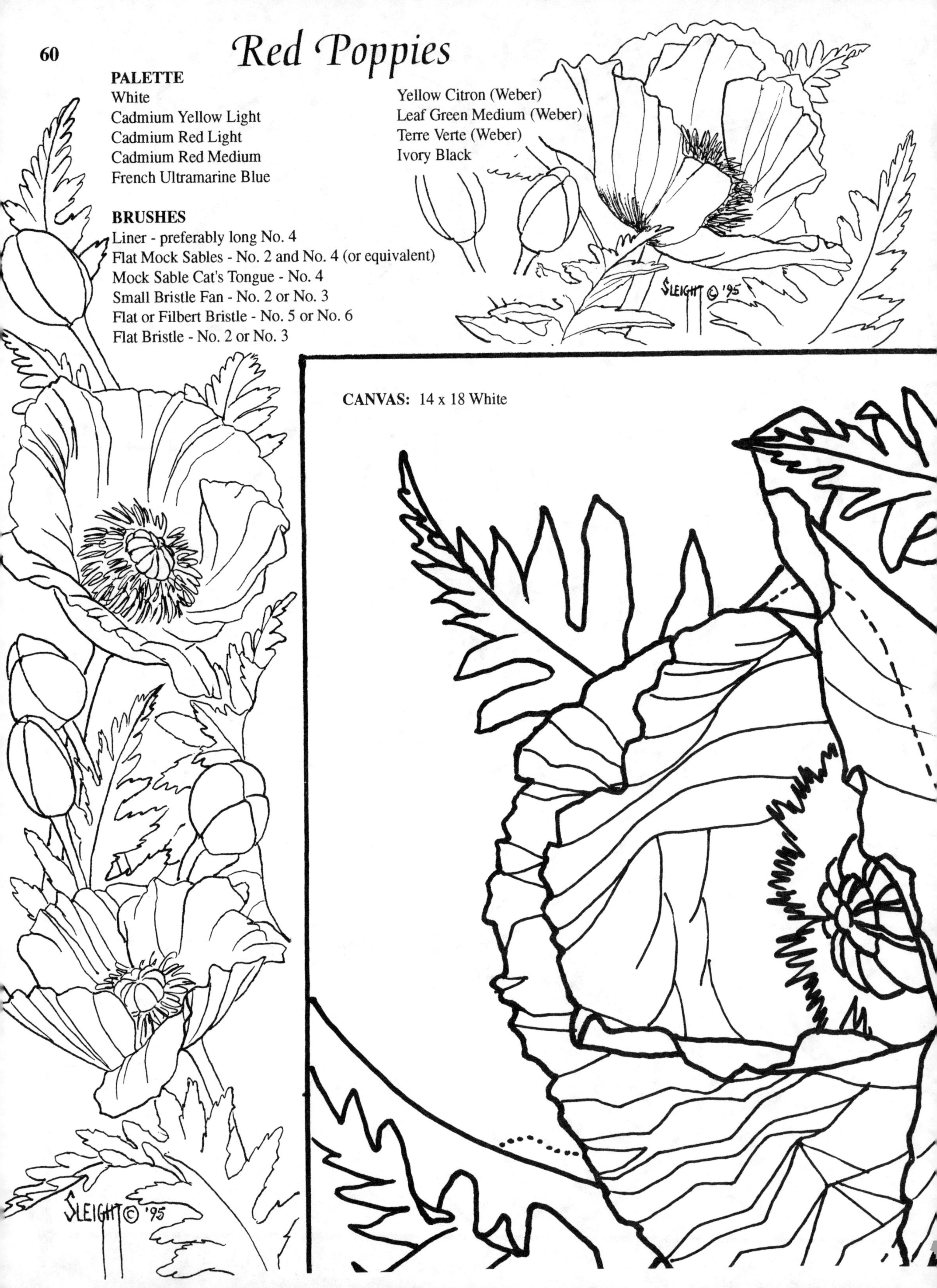



# Red Poppies

**PALETTE**

White
Cadmium Yellow Light
Cadmium Red Light
Cadmium Red Medium
French Ultramarine Blue

Yellow Citron (Weber)
Leaf Green Medium (Weber)
Terre Verte (Weber)
Ivory Black

**BRUSHES**

Liner - preferably long No. 4
Flat Mock Sables - No. 2 and No. 4 (or equivalent)
Mock Sable Cat's Tongue - No. 4
Small Bristle Fan - No. 2 or No. 3
Flat or Filbert Bristle - No. 5 or No. 6
Flat Bristle - No. 2 or No. 3

**CANVAS:** 14 x 18 White

**MEDIUMS**
Linseed Oil + Thinner or  (prepared medium WITHOUT drier)
Liquin - (Winsor & Newton product)

**MIX:**
Lt. Blue (1/2 tsp) ...........................White + French Ultramarine Blue + touch Cadmium Yellow Light.
Med. Blue (1/4 tsp) .......................White + more French Ultramarine Blue + touch Cadmium Yellow Light
Dk. Green No. 1 (1/2 tsp) ..............Terre Verte + French Ultramarine Blue
*Dk. Green No. 2 (1/2 tsp) ............Leaf Green Medium + French Ultramarine Blue
Med. Green No. 1 (1/2 tsp) ............Dark Green No. 2 + White + Yellow Citron
Med. Green No. 2 (1/2 tsp) ............Med. Green No. 1 + White + Yellow Citron
Lt. Green (1/4 tsp) ........................ Med. Green No. 2 + White + Yellow Citron
Highlight Green No. 1(1/4 tsp) .......Lt. Green + White + Yellow Citron
Highlight Green No. 2(1/8 tsp) .......Highlight Green No. 1 + White + Yellow Citron
    *Make a large pile of this to start (1 Tbsp) so you can make the lighter green mixes from it.

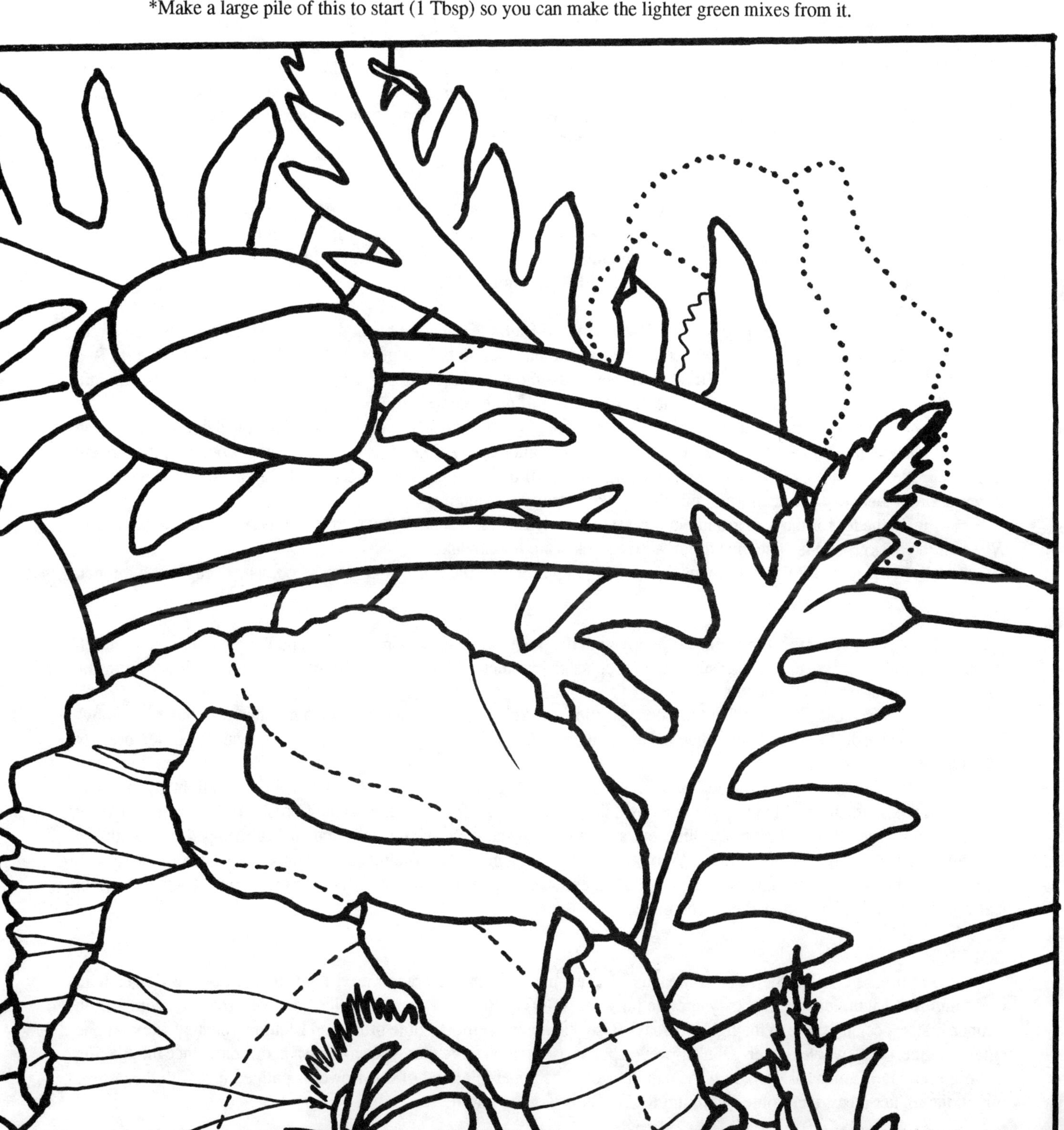

## Red Poppies continued

Transfer the pattern to your canvas using grey or black graphite paper. Note that the dotted lines refer to background poppies. The DASHED lines on the poppies are shadow lines.

### BACKGROUND

Start in the upper left corner with the lt. blue mix. Use a little medium (linseed oil + thinner) and a medium size No. 5 or No. 6 flat or filbert bristle brush. Keep the paint smooth, but not too thin. Leave spaces for the background poppies (and all the foreground flowers and leaves). Carry the lt. blue all across the top of the canvas, down below the buds on the left side and to the middle of the poppy on the right side.

Add some dk. green No. 1 to some med. blue mix with your brush. Using this mixture, overlap the lt. blue on the canvas. In some places suggest some leaf or bud shapes; other areas should just be loose strokes. Continue this across the canvas and down about to the top of the middle flower and about 1/2 way down the sides of the canvas still leaving spaces for the background poppies. As you progress further down the canvas, use more dk. green No. 1 and less med. blue. Where the background is lighter, work some lt. green mix into the blue/green shade (on the canvas).

Using a small fan brush or other small blender brush, soften what you have painted so far using a light X-stroke. Be careful not to go back into the lighter blue area after brushing the darker green areas unless you clean your brush and dry it well. Brush all the strokes horizontally across the canvas. Don't worry about paint that streaks across the foreground flowers - you will clean that off when the entire background is done.

### MIX:

Orange (1/4 tsp) ...........................................Cadmium Yellow Medium + Cadmium Red Light + White
Lt. Orange (1/8 tsp) .......................................Orange Mix + White + more Cadmium Yellow Light
Highlight Orange (1/8 tsp) .............................Light Orange + White + Cadmium Yellow Light
Dark Red (1/4 tsp) ........................................Cadmium Red Medium + Dk. Green No. 1

Paint in the background poppy using Cadmium Red Light, leaving the black center bare for now. Use the larger flat mock sable brush and Liquin. Leave cracks where the lines are until you get the shading in. Blend Cadmium Red Medium into the darker, shaded areas. Brush the orange mix into the brighter areas. Shade the lighter areas with Cadmium Red Medium. Shade the darker areas with the dk. red mix. Fill in the center with Ivory Black.

Let the red areas dry a little while you work on more of the background green areas. When the paint is tacky, brush each individual petal with your fan brush (use the corner in smaller areas). Then brush along the edges between the red and green area. Next brush very lightly across the whole canvas. If the red areas streak very much, brush <u>into</u> them instead of outward, or let them dry a little more. Finish all strokes going horizontally.

Finish the rest of the background in this same way, letting each section dry awhile, then brush with the fan brush. When all the background is done, make sure all the strokes are horizontal.

Clean the paint off the foreground leaves and poppies with a flat brush (one with a good chisel edge) and thinner.

### LEAVES

Fill in the two leaves above the left poppy with dk green No. 2 in the darkest areas and the medium greens and lt. green in the lighter areas. Use either small flat mock sable brush and Liquin. Brush lightly with the fan brush from the outside of the leaf towards the center.

Stipple (see definitions in front of book) a little "texture" look on the leaves with a medium size older "scrubby" brush. Use one shade darker or lighter than the original color, but no thick paint. This is just the appearance of texture, not actual texture.

Make a "softened pile" (see definitions) of some of the highlight green No. 1 and one of the highlight green No. 2. Use the highlight green No. 1 to paint the line down the center of the left leaf with your liner brush. Highlight the edges of the leaves with the same color. Add a little extra highlight on the parts of the right leaf that are flipped over with the highlight green No. 2. Add a little thinner to some of the highlight green No. 1 to make the hairs on the edges of the leaves. Use a liner brush with a good point and use very little pressure to get a very fine line. Make the hairs on the back of the right leaf in the same way, but with darker green mixes.

### POPPIES

Put a base coat on the lightest areas on the left poppy with the orange mix. Paint the rest of the flower with Cadmium Red Light, leaving cracks where the lines are. (NOTE: You may want to lighten some of the lines with a little thinner first, especially those in the lightest areas). Use the larger flat mock sable brush and Liquin. You may work on one petal at a time, or the whole flower. Don't however, put a base coat on more than you can finish in one day, since the shading and highlighting is much easier to do if the paint is wet. The upper left petal of this flower is painted first with the orange mix in the lighter areas, then some Cadmium Red Light is worked into it.

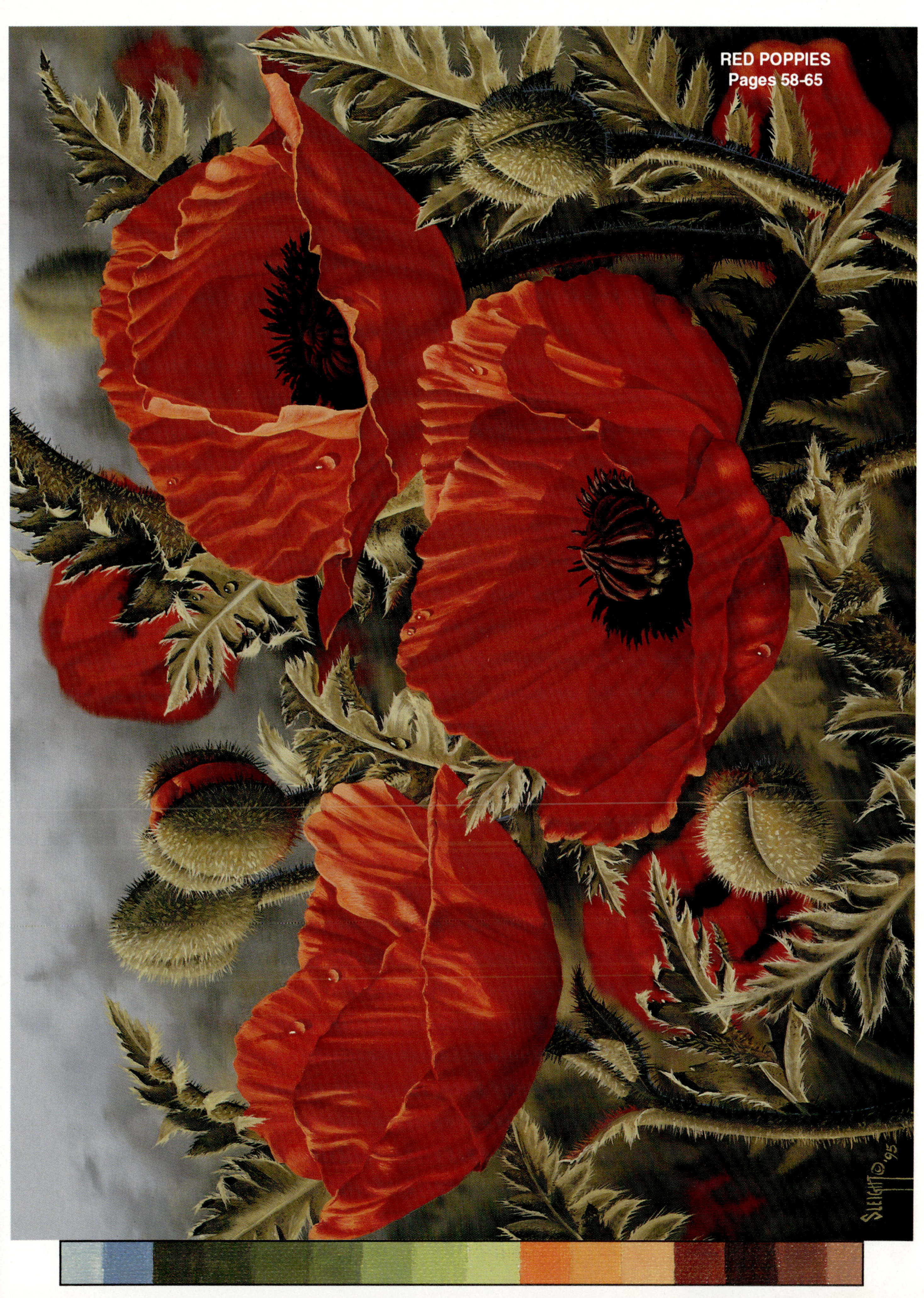
RED POPPIES
Pages 58-65
SLEIGHT © '95

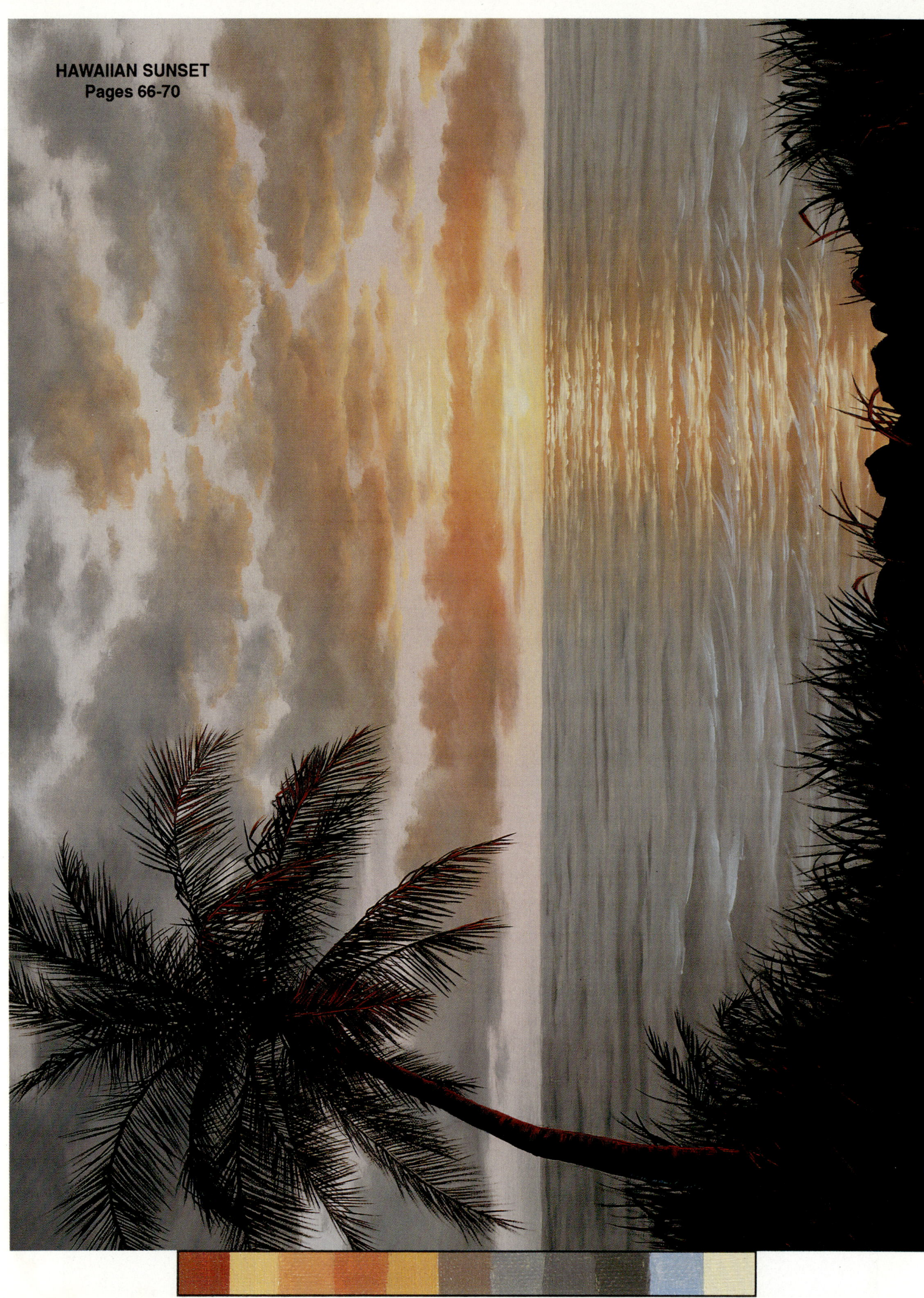
HAWAIIAN SUNSET
Pages 66-70

## Red Poppies continued

Blend Cadmium Red Medium into the Cadmium Red Light where it is darker. Your cat's tongue brush works well for this except along the edges. You don't need any more Liquin on the brush since the paint is already wet underneath.

Brush each petal with the fan brush, being careful not to brush over the lines between petals or other crisp shadow lines. Let this dry a little while you paint some more leaves or the upper buds.

After it has dried a little (should feel sticky), blend some dk. red mix into the darkest areas. You can vary this color a bit by adding more or less dk. green No. 1, but be careful not to use too much green or it will turn brown! Try not to have any dk. red color right next to the orange mix - always have some Cadmium Red Light in between as a transition color. Brush again with your fan brush.

Make a softened pile of some of your light orange mix. Use this to highlight the lighter areas of the petals and along some of the edges. Make a mini-fan (See Definitions) out of your long liner brush and brush over the highlights to soften or blend them a little (except along the edges where they appear as a line).

### BUDS

Fill in the green areas with the various green mixes as needed except the highlight greens. Use flat mock sable brushes and Liquin. Add some Yellow Citron into the lighter and middle tone areas. Paint the stems the same way. Brush with the fan brush, being careful not to brush over the edges. NOTE: Ignore the red and orange reflections on the buds and stems for now. They will be added when the paint is dry.

Soften with the fan brush. Paint the red area on the upper bud with Cadmium Red Light and Liquin. Shade it with Cadmium Red Medium and the dk. red mix, and highlight it with the orange mixes (not too light). Be sure to keep the lower part of it quite dark. If the paint is very slippery, wait awhile to do the shading and highlighting.

Let the buds dry quite a bit before adding the hairs (even completely dry if you want). Then paint the hairs as you did for the leaves. Start with the highlight green No. 2 on the left side, then gradually change to darker green as you move right. Be sure to add some thinner so you can get a very fine line. Note that the hairs get shorter as they approach the middle of the buds and then are just a dot in the middle.

On the two buds in the lower and right side of the picture, the lines between the sections are painted with the highlight green No. 1 and a little thinner. Where they are in shadow, use med. green No. 1 or lt. green with a little blue added. Be sure to paint these lines before you put the hairs on. For the brownish area on the "point" of the lower left bud, mix Cadmium Red Light + dk green No. 2 + Cadmium Yellow Light. Add White to this for the highlight. Or use Burnt Sienna and Burnt Sienna + White.

Add a backlight to the stems and the buds where necessary (where background is dark next to the dark side of the bud) use a darker shade of the med. blue mix (add French Ultramarine Blue). Use your liner brush and a little thinner. Blend this into the stem or bud a little so it doesn't look like a line. Proceed through the rest of the leaves and flowers in the same way. I like to work from left to right, since I'm right handed. I also prefer to paint a leaf that is behind another leaf or flower before I paint the one in front. That way you don't mess up the one on top trying to paint the one underneath.

### MIX:

Dk Brown (1/8 tsp) .........................Cadmium Red Medium + Ivory Black
Medium Brown (1/8 tsp) ................ Dk. Brown + White + Cadmium Red Light
Lt. Brown (1/8 tsp) ..........................Med. Brown + White + Cadmium Yellow Light

### POPPY CENTERS

Paint the black areas of the centers with Ivory Black. Use your smaller flat mock sable brush and Liquin. Fill in the darker red areas of the center with the dk. brown mix. Go over the brown areas on both the stamen and the middle area with the med. brown mix. The green area on the middle poppy is painted with the lt. green mix, then shaded with dk. green No. 2 and black.

Let this dry a bit, then highlight the green areas with highlight green No. 1, the brownish areas with the lt. brown mix, then the lt. orange mix. Put a backlight on the right side of the center with Cadmium Red Medium.

For the center on the upper right poppy, "highlight" the stamen and the middle with Cadmium Red Medium, then Cadmium Red Light (sparingly). In the middle, use the Cadmium Red Light only on the left side.

### WATERDROPS

Follow directions in front of book. Be careful not to get the colors too dark. On the flowers, the dark color should be Cadmium Red Medium or Cadmium Red Medium + just a touch of dk. green No. 1.

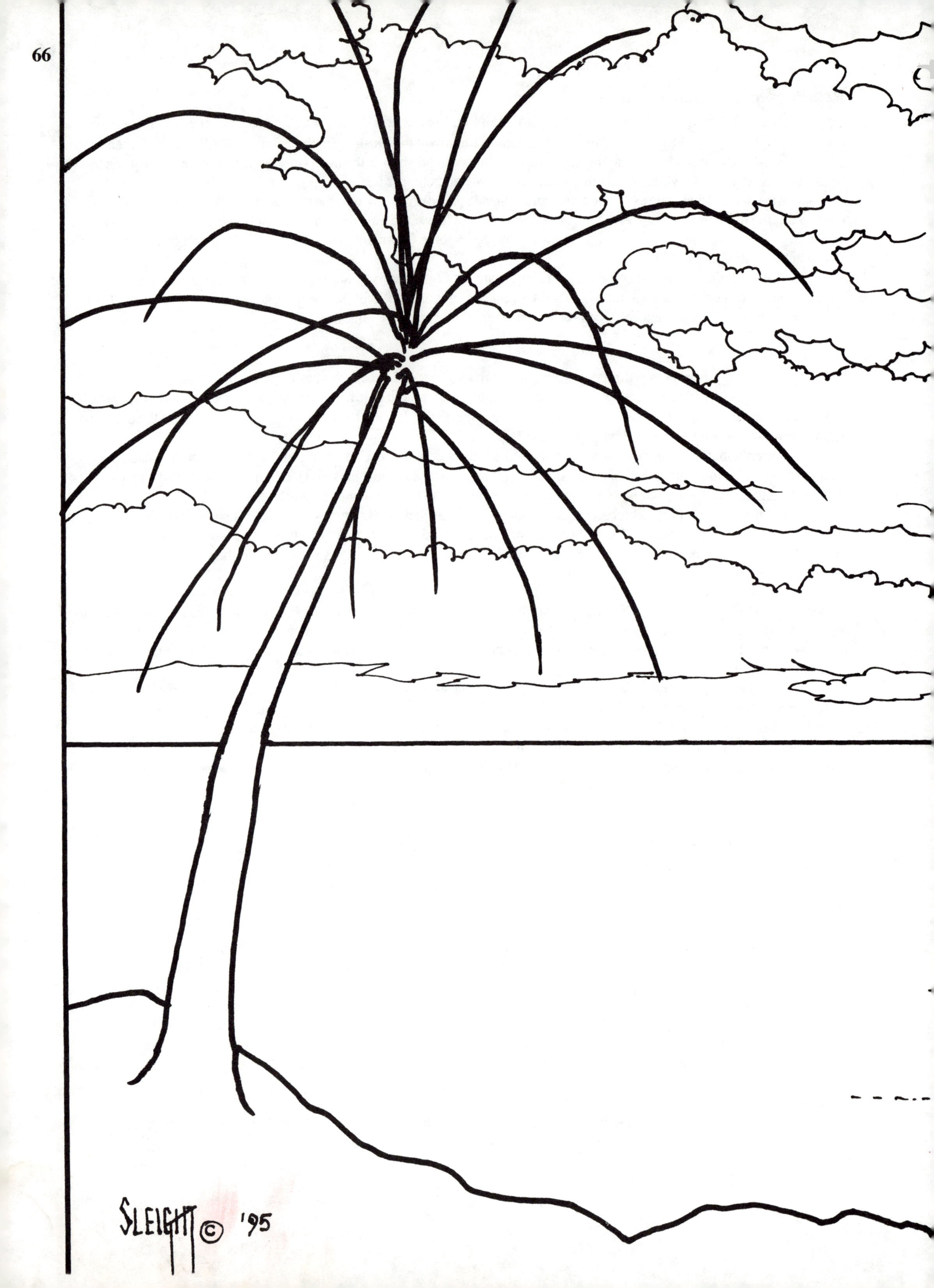
SLEIGHT © '95

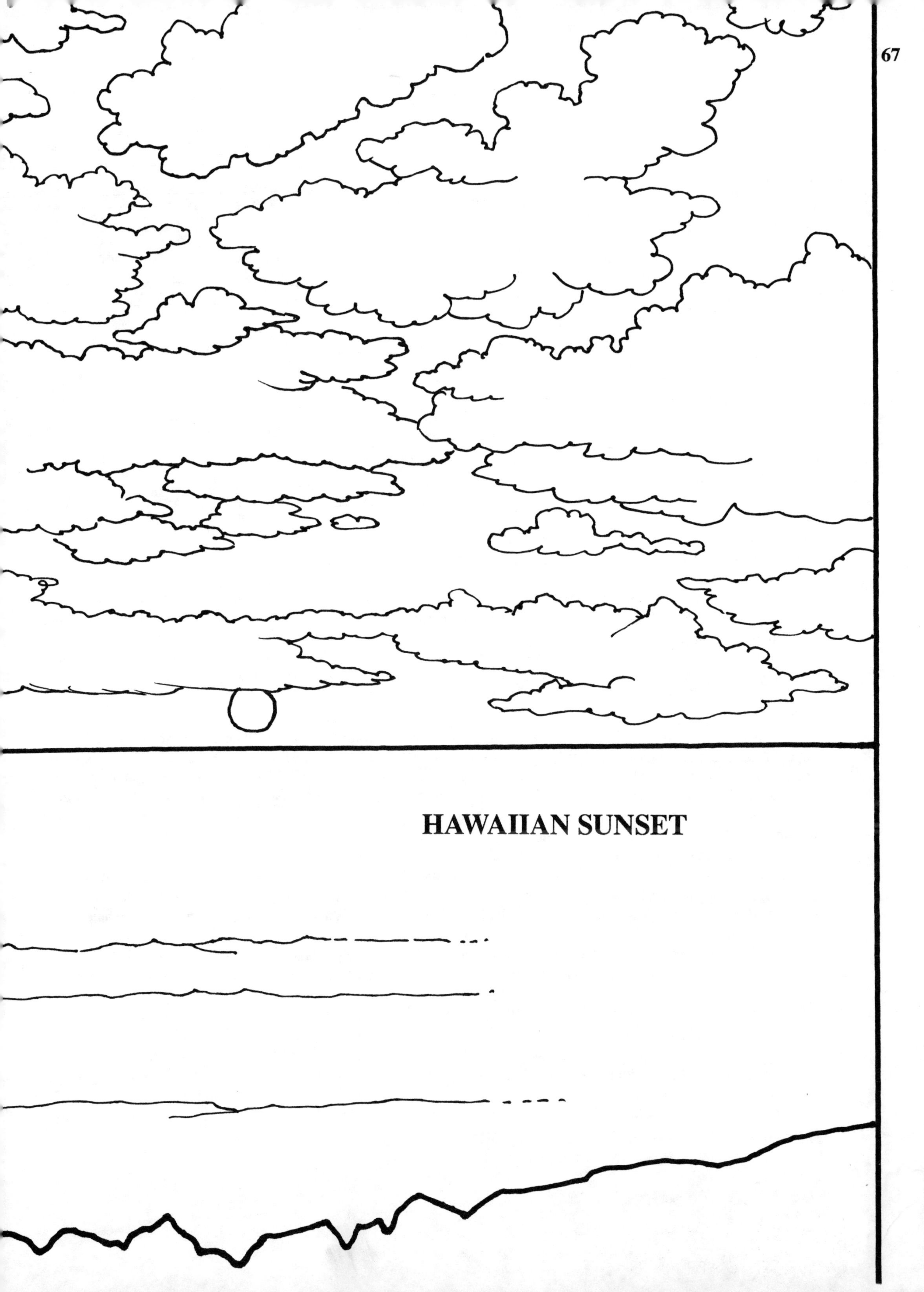

## HAWAIIAN SUNSET

# Hawaiian Sunset

**CANVAS:** 12 x 16 White

**PALETTE:**

| | |
|---|---|
| White | French Ultramarine Blue |
| Cadmium Yellow Light | Burnt Sienna |
| Grumbacher Red | Ivory Black |

**BRUSHES**
Liner - Preferable long No. 4
Flat Mock Sables - No. 2 and No. 4 (or equivalent)
Mock Sable Cat's Tongues - No. 4 and No. 6 or No. 8
Small Bristle Fan Brush - No. 2 or No. 3
Flat or Filbert Bristle Brush - No. 4 or No. 5
Optional - Sable Fan Brush - No. 2 or No. 3

**MEDIUMS:**
Liquin (Winsor & Newton)
Linseed Oil + Thinner ( or prepared medium WITHOUT a drier)

**MIX:**
Cream (1/2 tsp) ............................................. White + Cadmium Yellow Light
Light Blue (1/4 tsp) ..................................... White + French Ultramarine Blue

Transfer the pattern to your canvas using grey or black graphite paper . Try to keep the lines for the clouds very light. <u>DO NOT</u> trace the branches on the tree in yet; just the trunk. After the sky is dry, you can lay the pattern over it and trace on the branches.

Just before beginning to paint, erase the circle for the sun so you can barely see it. Be sure the eraser "bits" don't get into your paint! The short vertical line just below the horizon line and the sun should still be visible.

**SKY**

Cover the entire sky, <u>but not the clouds</u> with the cream mix. (Smaller clouds will be put in over the sky). Use a larger flat or cat's tongue mock sable brush or a No. 4 or No. 5 bristle brush and some Liquin. With a smaller flat mock sable brush and Cadmium Yellow Light (no more Liquin), draw a circle around the sun (about 3/8" in diameter) and about 1/8 inch above the horizon line. (The top of the sun is just under the clouds). Extend the Cadmium Yellow Light out to three inches beyond (and above) the sun. Change to a cat's tongue brush. Lay this brush on its side and blend the outer edges of the  yellow softly into the cream mix. Be sure to leave a crisp edge around the sun.

Get a small amount of Grumbacher Red on the cat's tongue brush, then wipe most of it off on your paper towel or rag. Overlap the yellow in the sky, starting about 1-1/2 inch on either side of the sun (and above), and extending all the way to the edges, letting it get paler (less red) as it gets further away. Clean the brush and dry it well. Laying it on its side, blend the red and yellow very lightly where they meet. Be careful not to carry this all the way up to the sun - use a lighter touch as you approach it.

Overlap the pink color with the lt. blue mix, starting at the outside edges of the canvas and working in toward the sun. This should get paler (less blue) as it gets closer to the sun and fade away completely by the time it's two or three inches away from the sun.

Add a touch more French Ultramarine Blue to some of the lt. blue mix. Paint this over the top and left sides of the sky, blending softly into the lighter color.

Using a small fan brush, blend the sky a little more and smooth out the brush strokes. Start around the sun with a semi-circular stroke, but don't blur the edges of the sun. Once you move out into the area with the blue in it, don't go back to the area around the sun without first cleaning the brush. When everything is sufficiently blended (no hard edges left except around the sun), brush all your strokes horizontally very lightly. Be sure to clean your brush before brushing across the sun.

## Hawaiian Sunset continued
### MIX:

Dk. Grey (3/4 tsp) ........................... White + Fr. Ultramarine Blue + Burnt Sienna (save about 1/8 tsp, mix  the medium grey with the rest)
Medium Grey (1/2 tsp) ................... Dark Grey + White
Light Grey (1/2 tsp) ........................ Medium Grey + White
Brownish-grey (1/4 tsp) ................. Light Grey + Burnt Sienna
Gold (1/8 tsp) ................................. Cream + Cadmium Yellow Light + touch Grumbacher Red + touch of  brownish grey
Orange (1/8 tsp) ............................. Gold + more Cadmium Yellow Light + more Grumbacher Red + brownish grey

### LOWEST CLOUDS

Using the smaller cat's tongue brush - on its side - start over the sun with the gold mix and Liquin (only enough to help the paint spread).  Continue this out about two inches on either side of the sun.  Overlap it with the orange mix and carry this out about another inch on either side.

Put in the smaller clouds over the sky as you go - when you have the right color on your brush.  When painting over wet paint, you don't need to use any more Liquin.

Add a little more Grumbacher Red and brownish-grey to some of the orange mix and continue a bit further away from the sun.  (Change to the larger cat's tongue brush if you'd like).  Use the brownish-grey mix (overlapping the reddish shade) for the rest of the cloud on the right and to approximately four inches from the left edge.  Fill in remaining part of this lower cloud with the light grey mix.

### UPPER CLOUDS

Start with the orange mix along the bottom of the second layer of clouds; change to the brownish-grey mix above.  Use the lt. grey mix when you're 4-1/2 to 5 inches away from the sun, then the med. grey as you approach the left upper corner and along the top of the canvas.

The clouds above that are brownish-grey above the sun, then lt. grey and med. grey as before.  Add some orange mix into the bottom of the upper cloud above the sun.  Work some dk. grey into the upper left corner and into the darker areas of the clouds on the left and upper sides.

Blend some white into the lighter areas of the first and second layer of clouds (mostly above the sun).

Don't spend too much time on the clouds behind the palm tree since they will be mostly covered  up by the tree.

Brush within the clouds with a small fan brush to soften and blend a little.  Work in the lighter clouds first and then stay out of them unless you clean your brush.

Clean the brush.  Using the corner, soften the edges of the clouds a little.  The clouds closest to the horizon  have the most crisp and clean edges.  As you move towards the top of the sky the edges get softer - more blurry.

Finish by brushing very lightly across the whole sky.  If the clouds streak over the sky, the paint may be too wet or your paint may be too thick.  If it's too thick, very lightly skim your knife across the canvas to remove some.  If it's too wet, wait awhile and try again.

### HIGHLIGHTED EDGES OF CLOUDS

Add White and Cadmium Yellow Light to some of the orange mix.  Use the small cat's tongue brush (no Liquin) - on its side - to add the highlights on the edges of the clouds.  Go back with a dry brush and feather the inside of the highlights up into the clouds.

Soften these highlights very slightly with a sable fan brush or your liner made into a "mini-fan" (see definitions in front of the book).

Mix a brighter orange shade with White + Cadmium Yellow Light +a  touch of Grumbacher Red.  Using the cat's tongue brush again, add extra highlights to the bottom of the second layer of clouds above the sun (this goes just below the previous highlight).  Add a little more Cadmium Yellow Light to some of the cream mix, then a few drops of medium (linseed oil + thinner).  Stir this in well with your knife.  Use a liner brush to add this highlight below the lowest bank of clouds and just above them.  Soften this highlight and the previous one with the mini-fan made from your liner brush.

Clean any paint off below the horizon line with a good chisel edge brush and thinner.  Be sure the horizon line is even (measure if necessary).  Where the tree crosses the horizon, clean off the paint a bit so there won't be any texture there.

### WATER

Using your larger flat mock sable brush, the gold mix and Liquin, make a vertical stripe below the sun about one inch wide and ending at the foreground rocks.  Be sure it is centered on the sun.  Paint very carefully at the horizon line to make a straight, even line.

On either side of the gold, make a stripe with the orange mix about 1/2 inch wide and slightly overlapping the gold stripe.

## Hawaiian Sunset continued

WATER continued

To blend these "stripes", stroke up and down with your brush (the same flat) while moving your hand to the right and left. If you start to drag too much orange over the gold, use less pressure on the brush as you go over the gold.

Overlap both sides of the orange with the brownish-grey mix, extending out at least another inch on each side. Then change to the lt. grey mix and carry it all the way to the right edge; on the left side change to the med. grey mix about half way across. Blend each change of colors as before.

Brush vertically with your fan brush, being careful not to mess up the horizon line. Finish with light, horizontal strokes across the whole canvas. Take one long stroke along the horizon line with the brush partly in the sky and partly in the water. Be very steady with this stroke to keep the horizon line straight.

Check to make sure the gold and orange "glow" is still evenly balanced under the sun.

With your larger flat mock sable brush (must have a good chisel edge) and the orange mix, make horizontal strokes (to simulate waves) across the gold area - very skinny and close together nearest the horizon, slightly thicker and further apart as they move down the canvas (no Liquin or medium).

Change to the lt. grey mix and continue the strokes out to the left and to the right, changing to the med. grey as soon as the lt. grey won't show up, then to the dk. grey on the left side only. These waves should not be continuous all the way to the edges, through. Break the strokes and start new ones - some short, some long, but all mostly straight until they get nearer the foreground. Even then they should not be too "bumpy".

Brush the water again with your fan brush - horizontally.

### HIGHLIGHTS ON WATER

Add a little more medium to the lightest highlight color (cream + yellow) you used on the clouds. Using your liner brush, highlight the tops of the waves directly under the sun. These should be short dots and dashes rather than continuous lines. Fill in a little between the waves. The highlights should be closer together when they are further away and should leave larger spaces for waves as they get closer. They should be about one inch wide near the horizon line, slightly wider at the bottom.

Add some medium to the bright orange color you mixed for cloud highlights. Extend the highlights on the tops of the waves a little further out on each side. Make a mini-fan out of your liner brush and pull the ends of the highlights out a bit. Brush very lightly over the highlights to soften just a little - more near the horizon, less near the bottom.

Add some thinner to the lt. blue mix with your liner brush and brush some strokes up (and to the right) onto the face of the two closest waves, and above some of the other closest waves in the darker areas. Put just a few strokes on the third wave back in the "orange" area.

### TREE AND FOREGROUND

Let the water and sky dry before painting the foreground and the tree. Transfer the pattern for the tree branches on over the sky.

Using your larger flat mock sable brush, Ivory Black and Liquin, fill in the grass and rocks in the foreground. Where there is grass, make the top irregular in shape; then turn the brush with the chisel edge vertical and push up the start of some grass. Come back with a liner brush, black and some thinner to make the individual grasses. The key to making the grasses skinny is to release pressure on the brush as you get to the top and pull away from the canvas.

Fill in the tree trunk with the smaller flat mock sable brush, black and Liquin.

Use your liner brush, black and thinner to put the palm fronds in. The paint must be very fluid, but not too thin or you'll get transparent or grey palms. Paint the highlighted ones black now - highlights will be added later.

Mix a darker shade of the orange mix by adding more Cadmium Yellow Light, Grumbacher Red and some dk. grey mix.

Add a fairly heavy line down the right side of the trunk with your liner brush and this darker orange shade (don't thin it down any more than necessary). Turn the painting sideways (to the left); make a narrow mini-fan out of your liner brush and pull this highlight across the trunk in <u>slightly</u> curved lines.

Darken some of the lt. blue mix with more French Ultramarine Blue. Put a backlight on the left side of the trunk near the bottom - only as far up as the grass is. Don't get this too light. Turn canvas to the right and pull this across the trunk in the same way as you did the highlight.

Use your liner brush, the darkened orange color and thinner to put highlights on some palm fronds on the right side of the tree (see picture).

Add some more grasses below the first ones using the darkened orange shade. These should not be too prominent - work them into the black a bit. Pull the bottom of these strokes down into the black, then add more black grasses below that. This should be done when the black undercoat has set up to a sticky stage, but <u>must</u> be done before the paint is dry.

Highlight the rocks with a small flat or cat's tongue brush and the darkened orange color when the black is almost dry. Pull a few grasses up under them.

# Susan Scheewe Publications, Inc.

## ACRYLIC BOOKS

| | | | |
|---|---|---|---|
| Vol. 19 | "Gift of Painting" by Susan Scheewe | 230 | $8.50____ |
| Vol. 1 | "Painting It's Our Bag" by Bev Hink/Susan Scheewe | 193 | $8.50____ |
| Vol. 4 | "Keepsake Sampler" by Susan & Camille Scheewe | 200 | $6.50____ |
| Vol. 1 | "Loving You" by Susan & Camille Scheewe | 244 | $7.50____ |
| Vol. 1 | "Keepsakes For The Holidays" by Charleen Stempel & Susan Scheewe | 286 | $8.50____ |
| Vol. 1 | "Mrs. MacGregor's Garden" by Charleen Stempel & Susan Scheewe | 316 | $8.50____ |
| Vol. 1 | "Kids And Water" by Joyce Benner | 234 | $8.50____ |
| Vol. 2 | "The Flower Market" by Joyce Benner | 319 | $8.50____ |
| Vol. 1 | "Natures Palette" by Carol Binford | 248 | $8.50____ |
| Vol. 1 | "Country Fixin's" by Rhonda Caldwell | 307 | $8.50____ |
| Vol. 2 | "Country Fixin's - Sunflower Friends" by Rhonda Caldwell | 321 | $8.50____ |
| Vol. 3 | "Country Fixin's - For All Seasons" by Rhonda Caldwell | 332 | $8.50____ |
| Vol. 1 | "Santas and Sams" by Bobi Dolara | 258 | $8.50____ |
| Vol. 2 | "Vintage Peace" by Bobi Dolara | 270 | $8.50____ |
| Vol. 1 | "Floral Designs" by Carol Empet | 312 | $8.50____ |
| Vol. 2 | "Floral Designs 2" by Carol Empet | 338 | $8.50____ |
| Vol. 1 | "Romantically Tole Bauernmalerei" by Sherry Gall | 311 | $8.50____ |
| Vol. 1 | "Holiday Gathering" by Angie Hupp | 267 | $8.50____ |
| Vol. 3 | "Heavenly Gathering" by Angie Hupp | 320 | $8.50____ |
| Vol. 1 | "Happy Heart, Happy Home" by Cathy Jones | 241 | $7.50____ |
| Vol. 1 | "Pickets & Pastimes" by Marie & Jim King | 329 | $8.50____ |
| Vol. 3 | "Country's Edge" by Shirley Koenig.....O/AC | 291 | $8.50____ |
| Vol. 1 | "Huckleberry Horse" by Hanna Long | 269 | $8.50____ |
| Vol. 1 | "Love Lives Here" by Mary Lynn Lewis | 170 | $6.50____ |
| Vol. 2 | "Love Lives Here" by Mary Lynn Lewis | 185 | $6.50____ |
| Vol. 3 | "Love Lives Here" by Mary Lynn Lewis | 195 | $6.50____ |
| Vol. 1 | "Special Welcomes" by Corinne Miller | 287 | $8.50____ |
| Vol. 2 | "Special Welcomes" by Corinne Miller | 298 | $8.50____ |
| Vol. 3 | "Special Welcomes #3, Crazy About Crafting" by Corinne Miller | 309 | $8.50____ |
| Vol. 4 | "Special Welcomes #4 Farm-N-Friends" by Corinne Miller | 324 | $8.50____ |
| Vol. 5 | "Special Welcomes #5 All Wrapped Up" by Corinne Miller | 333 | $8.50____ |
| Vol. 1 | "Change With The Seasons, Wire Loops" by Joanna Miller | 331 | $8.50____ |
| Vol. 1 | "Fruit & Flower Fantasies" by Joyce Morrison | 277 | $8.50____ |
| Vol. 1 | "Wildflower Sampler" by Bev Norman | 191 | $8.50____ |
| Vol. 1 | "Whimsical Critters" by Lori Ohlson | 228 | $7.50____ |
| Vol. 2 | "Sunflower Farm" by Lori Ohlson | 326 | $8.50____ |
| Vol. 1 | "Holiday Medley" by Nina Owens | 265 | $8.50____ |
| Vol. 2 | "Another Holiday Medley" by Nina Owens | 296 | $8.50____ |
| Vol. 1 | "Oh Those Little Rascals" by Diane Permenter | 247 | $7.50____ |
| Vol. 6 | "Acrylic Charms" by Sharon Rachal | 305 | $8.50____ |
| Vol. 1 | "Forever In My Heart" by Diane Richards.....AC/Fabric | 188 | $6.50____ |
| Vol. 2 | "Memories In My Heart" by Diane Richards.....AC/Fabric | 189 | $6.50____ |
| Vol. 3 | "Forever In My Heart II" by Diane Richards.....AC/Fabric | 205 | $7.50____ |
| Vol. 6 | "Angels In My Stocking" by Diane Richards | 254 | $7.50____ |
| Vol. 7 | "Nostalgic Dreams" by Diane Richards | 273 | $8.50____ |
| Vol. 1 | "Second Time Around" by Sally Sauermilch | 297 | $8.50____ |
| Vol. 2 | "Second Time Around" by Sally Sauermilch | 318 | $8.50____ |
| Vol. 1 | "Holiday Hangarounds" by Marsha Sellers | 327 | $8.50____ |
| Vol. 1 | "Creations In Canvas...and More" by Carol Spooner | 256 | $7.50____ |
| Vol. 1 | "Gran's Garden" by Ros Stallcup | 295 | $8.50____ |
| Vol. 2 | "Another Gran's Garden" by Ros Stallcup | 315 | $8.50____ |
| Vol. 3 | "Gran's Garden & House" by Ros Stallcup | 334 | $8.50____ |
| Vol. 1 | "Christmas Greetings from the Cottage" by Chris Stokes | 336 | $8.50____ |
| Vol. 1 | "Christmas Visions" by Max Terry | 278 | $8.50____ |
| Vol. 2 | "Christmas Presence" by Max Terry | 285 | $8.50____ |
| Vol. 3 | "Painting Clay Pot-pourri" by Max Terry | 310 | $8.50____ |
| Vol. 1 | "Country Primitives" by Maxine Thomas | 274 | $8.50____ |
| Vol. 2 | "Country Primitives 2" by Maxine Thomas | 300 | $8.50____ |
| Vol. 3 | "Country Primitives 3" by Maxine Thomas | 322 | $8.50____ |
| Vol. 1 | "Rise & Shine" by Jolene Thompson | 214 | $6.50____ |
| Vol. 2 | "Garden Gate" by Jolene Thompson | 250 | $7.50____ |
| Vol. 3 | "Count Your Blessings" by Chris Thornton | 196 | $6.50____ |
| Vol. 5 | "Count Your Blessings" by Chris Thornton | 213 | $8.50____ |
| Vol. 6 | "Share Your Blessings" by Chris Thornton | 226 | $8.50____ |
| Vol. 7 | "Blessings" by Chris Thornton | 255 | $8.50____ |
| Vol. 8 | "Christmas Blessings" by Chris Thornton | 266 | $8.50____ |
| Vol. 9 | "Blessings For The Home" by Chris Thornton | 275 | $8.50____ |
| Vol. 10 | "Bazaar Blessings" by Chris Thornton | 299 | $8.50____ |
| Vol. 11 | "Painted Blessings" by Chris Thornton | 323 | $8.50____ |
| Vol. 1 | "Watermelon Wedges and Rustic Edges" by Lorinne Thurlow | 342 | $8.50____ |
| Vol. 1 | "Barnyard Friends" by Lou Ann Trice | 306 | $8.50____ |
| Vol. 5 | "Daydreams & Sweet Shirts II" by Don & Lynn Weed | 208 | $7.50____ |
| Vol. 1 | "Connie's Favorite Old-Time Labels" by Connie Williams | 335 | $8.50____ |
| Vol. 1 | "Floral Fabrics and Watercolor" by Sally Williams | 262 | $8.50____ |
| Vol. 1 | "A Time For Giving" by Evelyn Wright | 308 | $8.50____ |

*******
SHIPPING &
HANDLING
CHARGES
Add $2.50 for the First Book for shipping and handling.

Add $1.50 per each additional book.

Please Add $3.00 for handling & postage. PER TAPES. <u>Sorry we must have a "NO RE-FUND - NO RETURN" policy.</u>

U.S CURRENCY

PRICES SUBJECT TO CHANGE WITHOUT NOTICE.

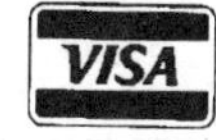 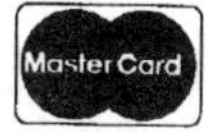

WE GLADLY ACCEPT VISA & MASTERCARD

FOR MORE INFORMATION ON BOOKS OR SUPPLIES CALL OR WRITE US

WE ARE ALWAYS GLAD TO HEAR FROM YOU!

11-21-95

13435 N.E. Whitaker Way  Portland, Or. 97230  PH (503) 254-9100  FAX (503) 252-9508

## WATERCOLOR BOOKS

| Vol. 20 | "Simply Country Watercolors" by Susan Scheewe Brown | 257 | $8.50 ___ |
| Vol. 21 | "Simply Watercolor" by Susan Scheewe Brown.....T.V. Book | 260 | $11.95 ___ |
| Vol. 22 | "Watercolor For Everyone" by Susan Scheewe Brown.....T.V. Book | 276 | $11.95 ___ |
| Vol. 23 | "Watercolor Step by Step" by Susan Scheewe Brown.....T.V. Book | 294 | $11.95 ___ |
| Vol. 24 | "Introduction to Watercolor" by Susan Scheewe Brown.....T.V. Book | 314 | $11.95 ___ |
| Vol. 25 | "Watercolors Anyone Can Paint" by Susan Scheewe Brown...T.V. Book | 324 | $11.95 ___ |
| Vol. 26 | "Watercolor - The Garden Scene" by Susan Scheewe Brown... T.V. Book | 341 | $11.95 ___ |
| Vol. 4 | "Enjoy Watercolor" by Ellie Cook | 210 | $7.50 ___ |
| Vol. 6 | "Watercolor Memories" by Ellie Cook | 246 | $8.50 ___ |
| Vol. 7 | "My Favorite Things In Watercolor" by Ellie Cook | 293 | $8.50 ___ |
| Vol. 3 | "Watercolor Made Easy 3" by Kathy George | 301 | $8.50 ___ |
| Vol. 1 | "The Way I Started" by Gary Hawk | 120 | $6.00 ___ |
| Vol. 2 | "Anyone Can Watercolor" by Ken Johnson | 118 | $6.50 ___ |
| Vol. 1 | "Watercolor Fun & Easy" by Beverly Kaiser | 243 | $7.50 ___ |
| Vol. 1 | "Flowers, Ribbon and Lace in Watercolor" by Linda McCulloch | 280 | $8.50 ___ |

## PEN & INK BOOKS / COLORED PENCIL BOOKS

| Vol. 6 | "Journey of Memories" by Claudia Nice | 166 | $6.50 ___ |
| Vol. 7 | "Scenes from Seasons Past" by Claudia Nice | 183 | $8.50 ___ |
| Vol. 8 | "Taste of Summer" by Claudia Nice | 223 | $8.50 ___ |
| Vol. 9 | "Familiar Faces" by Claudia Nice | 284 | $8.50 ___ |
| Vol. 2 | "Colored Pencil Made Easy" by Jane Wunder | 242 | $7.50 ___ |
| Vol. 3 | "The Beauty of Colored Pencil and Ink Drawing" by Jane Wunder | 259 | $7.50 ___ |

## VIDEOS BY SUSAN SCHEEWE BROWN

| "The Gift Of Painting Simply Watercolor" 60 Minutes | $24.95 ___ |
| "The Gift Of Painting" 90 Minutes | $24.95 ___ |
| "Paintings For The Holidays" 60 Minutes | $24.95 ___ |
| "Watercolor & Oil Do Mix" 60 Minutes | $24.95 ___ |
| "Watercolor Special Effects" 60 Minutes | $24.95 ___ |

NAME ______________________

______________________

ADDRESS ______________________

______________________

CITY/STATE/ZIP ______________________

______________________

PH( ) ______________________

VISA ______________________

M/C ______________________

EXP. DATE ______________________

SHIPPING $ ______________________

SHIP TO ______________________

______________________

______________________

## ——— OILS BOOKS ———

| Vol. 1 | "His and Hers" by Susan Scheewe | 101 | $6.50 ___ |
| Vol. 6 | "Brushed With Elegance" by Susan Scheewe | 106 | $5.50 ___ |
| Vol. 7 | "Paint 'n Patch" by Susan Scheewe | 107 | $5.50 ___ |
| Vol. 11 | "I Love To Paint" by Susan Scheewe | 111 | $6.50 ___ |
| Vol. 14 | "Enjoy Painting Animals" by Susan Scheewe | 114 | $6.50 ___ |
| Vol. 17 | "Countryside Reflections" by Susan Scheewe | 161 | $6.50 ___ |
| Vol. 19 | "Gift Of Painting" by Susan Scheewe O/AC/WC | 230 | $8.50 ___ |
| Vol. 1 | "Western Images" by Becky Anthony | 186 | $6.50 ___ |
| Vol. 3 | "Fantasy Flowers II" by Georgia Bartlett | 129 | $6.50 ___ |
| Vol. 4 | "Soft Petals" by Georgia Bartlett | 171 | $6.50 ___ |
| Vol. 6 | "Painting Fantasy Flowers" by Georgia Bartlett | 215 | $7.50 ___ |
| Vol. 7 | "Flowers" by Georgia Bartlett | 290 | $8.50 ___ |
| Vol. 8 | "Petals" by Georgia Bartlett | 317 | $8.50 ___ |
| Vol. 2 | "Painting, a Barrel of Fun" by Donna Bell | 201 | $7.50 ___ |
| Vol. 3 | "Barnscapes & More" by Donna Bell | 218 | $8.50 ___ |
| Vol. 4 | "Countryscapes" by Donna Bell | 249 | $8.50 ___ |
| Vol. 5 | "Painter to Painter" by Donna Bell | 263 | $8.50 ___ |
| Vol. 6 | "Landscapes With Acrylics & Oil" by Donna Bell | 282 | $8.50 ___ |
| Vol. 1 | "Natures Palette" by Carol Binford.....O/AC | 248 | $8.50 ___ |
| Vol. 1 | "Oil Painting The Easy Way" by Bill Blackman | 219 | $8.50 ___ |
| Vol. 2 | "Oil Painting The Easy Way" by Bill Blackman | 337 | $8.50 ___ |
| Vol. 1 | "Mini Mini More" by Terri and Nancy Brown | 150 | $6.50 ___ |
| Vol. 2 | "Mini Mini More" by Terri and Nancy Brown | 151 | $6.50 ___ |
| Vol. 4 | "Heritage Trails" by Terri and Nancy Brown | 169 | $6.50 ___ |
| Vol. 6 | "Garden Trails" by Terri and Nancy Brown | 283 | $8.50 ___ |
| Vol. 2 | "Windows of My World" by Jackie Claflin | 181 | $7.50 ___ |
| Vol. 3 | "Windows of My World 3" by Jackie Claflin | 303 | $8.50 ___ |
| Vol. 1 | "Expressions In Oil" by Delores Egger | 154 | $6.50 ___ |
| Vol. 4 | "Expressions In Oil" by Delores Egger | 239 | $7.50 ___ |
| Vol. 1 | "Victorian Days" by Gloria Gaffney | 240 | $8.50 ___ |
| Vol. 2 | "Days of Heaven" by Gloria Gaffney | 252 | $8.50 ___ |
| Vol. 3 | "Winter Song" by Gloria Gaffney | 271 | $8.50 ___ |

| Vol. 1 | "Roses Are For Everyone" by Bill Huffaker | 145 | $7.50 |
| Vol. 3 | "Nature's Beauty" by Bill Huffaker | 177 | $6.50 |
| Vol. 1 | "Copper, Silver, Brass & Glass" by Susan Jenkins | 211 | $6.50 |
| Vol. 1 | "In Full Bloom" by Susan Jenkins | 313 | $8.50 |
| Vol. 1 | "Backroads of My Memory" by Geri Kisner | 225 | $7.50 |
| Vol. 2 | "Backroads of My Memory" by Geri Kisner | 245 | $7.50 |
| Vol. 3 | "Country's Edge" by Shirley Koenig.....O/AC | 291 | $8.50 |
| Vol. 1 | "Ducks and Geese" by Jean Lyles | 172 | $6.50 |
| Vol. 1 | "Raining Cats & Dogs" by Todd Mallett | 304 | $8.50 |
| Vol. 1 | "Pathway To Painting" by Lee McGowan | 281 | $8.50 |
| Vol. 2 | "Another Path To Follow" by Lee McGowen | 328 | $8.50 |
| Vol. 1 | "Bitterroot Backroads" by Glenice Moore | 330 | $8.50 |
| Vol. 2 | "Bitteroot Backroads 2" by Glenice Moore | 340 | $8.50 |
| Vol. 1 | "Stepping Stones" by Judy Nutter | 121 | $6.50 |
| Vol. 1 | "Rustic Charms" by Sharon Rachal | 175 | $6.50 |
| Vol. 2 | "Rustic Charms II" by Sharon Rachal | 199 | $7.50 |
| Vol. 3 | "Rustic Charms III" by Sharon Rachal | 217 | $6.50 |
| Vol. 4 | "Rustic Charms IV" by Sharon Rachal | 238 | $7.50 |
| Vol. 5 | "Rustic Charms V, Florals" by Sharon Rachal | 261 | $8.50 |
| Vol. 1 | "Painting Flowers With Augie" by Augie Reis | 152 | $6.50 |
| Vol. 2 | "Painting Realism" by Judy Sleight | 272 | $8.50 |
| Vol. 3 | "Realistic Technique" by Judy Sleight | 341 | $8.50 |
| Vol. 1 | "Soft & Misty Paintings" by Kathy Snider | 204 | $8.50 |
| Vol. 2 | "Soft & Misty Paintings" by Kathy Snider | 229 | $8.50 |
| Vol. 2 | "More Old Friends" by Gene Waggoner | 148 | $6.50 |
| Vol. 4 | "Friends We've Known" by Gene Waggoner | 187 | $7.50 |
| Vol. 5 | "Friends Are Forever" by Gene Waggoner | 231 | $7.50 |
| Vol. 1 | "Fantasy Folk" by Don Weed | 123 | $6.50 |
| Vol. 2 | "Painting The Clowns" by Don Weed | 124 | $6.50 |
| Vol. 1 | "Something Special For Everyone" by Mildred Yeiser | 158 | $6.50 |
| Vol. 2 | "Something Special For Everyone" by Mildred Yeiser | 178 | $6.50 |
| Vol. 5 | "Soft & Gentle Paintings" by Mildred Yeiser | 268 | $8.50 |

*Susan Scheewe Publications Inc.*
13435 N.E. Whitaker Way  Portland, Or. 97230  PH (503)254-9100  FAX (503)252-9508